CHILDREN AND FAMILIES

Paul Michael Garrett,

with responses from Rona Woodward, Mark Drakeford and Ian
Butler, Donna Baines, Roger Smith, Stanley Houston, Griet Roets
and Rudi Roose, and Fabian Kessl

SERIES EDITORS:
Iain Ferguson and Michael Lavalette

D0299775

This print edition first published in Great Britain in 2014 by

Policy Press
University of Bristol
6th Floor
Howard House
Queen's Avenue
Bristol BS8 1SD
UK
t: +44 (0)117 331 5020
f: +44 (0)117 331 5367
pp-info@bristol.ac.uk
www.policypress.co.uk

North American office:
Policy Press
c/o The University of Chicago Press
1427 East 60th Street
Chicago, IL 60637, USA
t: +1 773 702 7700
f: +1 773-702-9756
e:sales@press.uchicago.edu
www.press.uchicago.edu

Edition history: first published digitally in 2013

ISBN 978 1 44731 619 0 paperback

British Library Cataloguing in Publication Data
A catalogue record for this book is available from the British Library.

Library of Congress Cataloging-in-Publication Data
A catalog record for this book has been requested.

The right of Paul Michael Garrett to be identified as author of this work has been asserted by him in accordance with the Copyright, Designs and Patents Act 1988.

The statements and opinions contained within this publication are solely those of the contributors and not of the University of Bristol or Policy Press. The University of Bristol and Policy Press disclaim responsibility for any injury to persons or property resulting from any material published in this publication.

Every effort has been made to trace copyright holders and to obtain their permission for the use of copyright material. The publisher apologises for any errors or omissions in the text and would be grateful if notified of any corrections that should be incorporated in future reprints or editions of this book.

Policy Press works to counter discrimination on grounds of gender, race, disability, age and sexuality.

Cover design Policy Press
Printed in Great Britain by www.4edge.co.uk

OTHER TITLES AVAILABLE IN THIS SERIES

POVERTY AND INEQUALITY by Chris Jones and Tony Novak

PERSONALISATION by Peter Beresford

ADULT SOCIAL CARE by Iain Ferguson and Michael Lavalette

MENTAL HEALTH by Jeremy Weinstein

ETHICS by Sarah Banks

For more information about this series visit: www.policypress.co.uk/crdsw.asp

Policy Press also publishes the journal *Critical and Radical Social Work*; for more information visit: http://www.policypress.co.uk/journals_crsw.asp

Contents

Notes on contributors

Lead author

Paul Michael Garrett is a senior lecturer at the National University of Ireland, Galway. He is the author of four single-authored books critically examining social work/social policy relating to children and families: *Remaking social work with children and families* (Routledge, 2003); *Social work with Irish children and families in Britain* (Policy Press, 2004); *'Transforming' children's services?* (Open University/McGraw Hill, 2009); *Social work and social theory* (Policy Press, 2013).

Respondents

Rona Woodward is a lecturer in social work at the University of Stirling. She is a founder member of the Social Work Action Network and author (with Iain Ferguson) of *Radical social work in practice* (Bristol, Policy Press).

Mark Drakeford is Professor of Social Policy and Applied Social Sciences, Cardiff University, and a Member of the National Assembly for Wales. Among his many publications is: (with Ian Butler) *Social work on trial: the Maria Colwell Inquiry and the state of welfare*, Bristol, Policy Press.

Ian Butler is Professor and Acting Dean of the Faculty of Humanities & Social Sciences, University of Bath. He is a qualified social worker with considerable practice and managerial experience. He has worked in residential and field settings, mainly with children and their families, in the statutory, voluntary and independent sectors.

Donna Baines is Professor, Labour Studies Programme and School of Social Work, and Chair of the Work and Society Graduate Program at McMaster University, Ontario, Canada

—

Roger Smith is Professor of Social Work at Durham University. Among his many publications is *Doing justice to young people: youth crime and social justice* (New York: Willan/Routledge).

Stanley Houston is Professor of Social Work at Queen's University Belfast. He worked in child and family social work for around 20 years before entering higher education in 1997. His main research interest lies in the application of critical social theory to social work .

Griet Roets is a senior researcher affiliated to the Department of Social Welfare Studies, Ghent University, Belgium. She has a PhD in educational sciences. Her research interests are poverty, gender, critical disability studies, critical social work and narrative and ethnographic research.

Rudi Roose works and researches at Ghent University, Belgium. He has written widely on various aspects of children's lives, childhood, education, social work and poverty.

Fabian Kessl is Professor for Theory and Practice of Social Work at the University of Duisburg-Essen, Germany. He is on the Advisory Board of *Neue Praxis* and is Chief Executive Officer of the online-only journal *Social Work & Society*.

Series editors

Iain Ferguson is Professor of Social Work and Social Policy at the University of the West of Scotland and a member of the Steering Committee of the Social Work Action Network.

Michael Lavalette is Professor of Social Work and Social Policy at Liverpool Hope University and National Co-ordinator of the Social Work Action Network.

Series editors' introduction

For much of its history, mainstream social work in Britain has been a fairly conservative profession. It has often reflected the dominant political ideologies of the day, while presenting itself as resolutely 'non-political'. Thus, the first social work organisation, the Charity Organisation Society (COS) (1869), rigorously adhered to the Poor Law notion that the poor could be divided into 'deserving' and 'undeserving', rejected any form of state intervention aimed at improving people's lives (including free school meals and old-age pensions) and saw the practice of individual casework as the best antidote to the spread of socialist ideas.

By contrast, social work in the 1960s reflected a broad social democratic consensus, evident in the recommendations of the Seebohm Report in England and Wales and the Kilbrandon Report in Scotland on the basis of which the new generic social work departments were established. In most respects, the social work of this period reflected a huge advance on the punitive individualism of the COS (and, it should be said, the punitive individualism of our own time). Even then, however, there was still a tendency to pathologise (albeit it was communities rather than individuals that were seen as failing) and to ignore the extent to which statutory social work intervention continued to be experienced by service users as oppressive and paternalistic. Be that as it may, the progressive possibilities of the new departments were soon cut short by the onset of a global economic crisis in 1973 to which the Labour governments of the time could offer no answer, except cuts and belt-tightening.

What is also true, however, as we have argued elsewhere (Lavalette and Ferguson, 2007), is that there has always been another tradition in social work, an activist/radical approach which has sought to present an alternative vision both to individualism and also to paternalist, top-down collectivism. This approach, which flourished in the UK in the 1970s, located the problems experienced by those who sought social work support in the material conditions of their lives and attempted to develop practice responses that challenged these conditions and their effects.

One source of theory underpinning that approach was the excellent series Critical Texts in Social Work and the Welfare State, edited by Peter Leonard and published by Macmillan.

Three decades on, this current series aims to similarly deepen and refresh the critical and radical social work tradition by providing a range of critical perspectives on key issues in contemporary social work. Social work has always been a contested profession but the need for a space for debate and discussion around ways forward for those committed to a social work practice informed by notions of social justice has never been greater. The issues are complex. How should social workers view personalisation, for example? In an era of austerity, can social work be about more than simply safeguarding and rationing scarce services? Will the integration of services in areas such as mental health lead to improved services or simply greater domination of medical models? Do social work practices offer an escape from managerialism and bureaucracy or are they simply a Trojan horse for privatisation?

These are some of the questions which contributors to this series – academics, practitioners, service users and movement activists – will address. Not all of those contributing to these texts would align themselves with the critical or radical tradition. What they have in common, however, is a commitment to a view of social work which is much wider than the currently dominant neoliberal models and a belief that notions of human rights and social justice should be at the heart of the social work project.

Children and families: Paul Michael Garrett

In this book within the series Paul Michael Garrett introduces a comparative analysis of child protection systems in England and the Republic of Ireland. In both countries governments committed to neoliberalism are bringing about significant, transformative changes to the welfare systems and to child protection regimes.

Garrett utilises a broadly Gramscian approach to offer an analysis of the changes taking place and their impact on social workers and social work service users. In the commentaries that accompany the lead essay authors from across Europe and North America engage with Garrett's thesis and offer an insight into welfare changes and child protection transformations within the nation state where they are located.

Radical and critical perspectives on social work with children and families: England and the Republic of Ireland

Paul Michael Garrett

England and the Republic of Ireland are bound together historically and in a contemporary sense. Both are currently governed by coalition administrations intent on pursing broadly neoliberal policies. In terms of social work practice, in the Republic, the main legislation relating to social work with children was, until the enactment of the Children Act 2001, the Children Act 1908 placed on the statute book by the former British colonial administration. Today, social work in both England and Ireland is mostly work undertaken by women workers. In the latter jurisdiction, 83.2% of social work posts are filled by women (NSWQB, 2006, p 23). Nevertheless, not surprisingly, there are certain national defining characteristics. That is to say, the difficulties and dilemmas confronting practitioners, social work academics and the users of services are not the same in England and the Republic of Ireland.

This relatively short contribution to the 'Radical and Critical Perspectives' series can only begin to identify some of the main emerging issues and themes relating to social work with children and families.[1] In this context, readers need to be alert to the fact that it is, I feel, misguided to simply view social work – with children and families or any other group – as an entirely benign and emancipatory

–

activity. Social work should not be sentimentalised and its function and purpose misunderstood. When discussing social work, we need to keep the state in vision: by and large, social workers are employed by the state and this is a social formation that does not simply act as a 'good-enough parent', seeking to intervene in the lives of children because of the need to ensure that their welfare is 'paramount'. The state, in both England and the Republic of Ireland, is not socially or economically neutral and its fundamental role is to maintain the present ordering of economic relations. As Bourdieu (2001, p 34) has elaborated, the state is:

> an ambiguous reality. It is not adequate to say that it is an instrument in the hands of the ruling class. The state is certainly not completely neutral, completely independent of the dominant forces in society, but the older it is and the greater the social advances it has incorporated the more autonomous it is. It is a battlefield.

Related to this perspective, as Parton (2000, p 457) observed a number of years ago:

> [one of] social work's enduring characteristics seems to be its essentially contested and ambiguous nature.... Most crucially, this ambiguity arises from a commitment to individuals and families and their needs on the one hand and its allegiances to and legitimation by the state in the guise of the courts and its 'statutory' responsibilities on the other.

Presently, we are enduring a 'conservative revolution' (Bourdieu, 2001) and this is also determining the shape and core objectives of the state. More expansively, we are living in a period in which processes of neoliberalisation continue to impact on, and to *remake*, all areas of life.

Importantly, how the agenda of neoliberalisation is assembled and amplified is connected to the roles of strategically placed individuals. In this sense, the diffusion of neoliberal ideas is not the result of the machinations of 'faceless, structural forces' (Peck, 2004, p 399); rather, structurally positioned agents are immensely important in terms of how they seek to formulate and promote such ideas and establish a new 'common sense'. Academics and consultants, as well as politicians, are playing a key role in articulating 'change' and in providing an 'expert' and (contentiously) 'independent' foundation for policy departures impacting on social work with children and families. In England, the London School of Economics and Political Science (LSE) has provided an ideas factory for 'modernisation' within and beyond Children's Services: Giddens (1998), of course, was the intellectual architect of New Labour's neoliberalism and he was to find a champion in social work's academic literature in Harry Ferguson (2001). Other academics based at the LSE, such as Julian Le Grand (2007) and Eileen Munro (Department of Education, 2011), although far from being entirely at one in their vision for change, continue to function as organic intellectuals of the current Coalition's 'transformation' agenda by furnishing plans, programmes and reports that map the reorientation of social work and related services. On the other side of the Irish Sea, key architects of 'transformation' include Frances Fitzgerald, the current Minister for Children, and also Gordon Jeyes, a former Director of Children's Services in the UK, who was appointed by the Health Services Executive (HSE) as the National Director for Children and Family Services in the Republic. Such figures help to create the 'spirit' of 'reform' and to enlist and retain the allegiance of practitioners during a period when fractured welfare states denude social workers of resources (see also Boltanski and Chiapello, 2005). Part of this project strategically pivots on the need to eliminate counter-perspectives or untidy elements that do not fit within the 'change agenda'.

Underpinning this contribution to the series, therefore, is the Gramscian idea that there is a need to focus on the molecular details associated with the project to create a new hegemony in the sector.[2] This approach leads us to pose a number of questions about changes being promoted within Children's Services in England and the Republic of Ireland. The tonality and texture of the 'reform' discourse is not the same in these jurisdictions and it operates within different professional, expert and emotional registers, but the focal questions include: how are vaunted 'new' ideas and plans related to older forms of thinking and acting within the sector? How is the private sector beginning to play a more substantial role? How is the case for 'reform' being made and orchestrated? Which groups are operating as the primary definers, providing a critique of the 'way things are' and mapping the 'way things should be'? What are the patterns of association and political and professional adherences of those promoting 'reform'? What are the new shapes of control and regulation that are emerging? What are the new surveillance practices that are now evolving, which are being directed at both the users of services and the providers of services? What are the sources of resistance? Clearly, such questions are rarely central in social work education and practice, but, in what follows, it will be maintained that being critically aware is vital in these turbulent times.

England

Hemmed in by 'neoliberal rationality': reviewing New Labour (1997–2010)

It is vital to try to identify some of the key components of New Labour policymaking impacting on social work with children and families because this continues to provide a foundation for the interventions of the current Conservative–Liberal Democrat Government that came to power in 2010. A number of years into the period of New Labour governments (1997–2010), I observed in my book *Remaking social work with children and families* (Garrett, 2003, p 139) that 'social work is always, in a sense, being *re-made* and it is not possible to have nervous recourse to an authentic or timeless form of practice. Social work is always changing and evolving into something else, always *in process*'. At this time, a key characteristic of social work with children and families included the creation of new structures, such as Children's Trusts, a panoply of new regulatory and inspection bodies, and a range of new agencies, such as the Youth Justice Board and Youth Offending Teams. New Labour was driven by the aspiration to embed multidisciplinary working and 'joined-up' approaches. This was apparent in the Crime and Disorder Act 1998 and the Children Act 2004. The New Labour administrations, perhaps especially the initial one formed in 1997, displayed tremendous reforming energy. Oftentimes, this contained the residues of a progressive politics; more frequently, it pivoted on a commitment at the top of the party to 'roll-with-it neoliberalization' (Keil, 2009).

Political 'spin' played a key role in promoting and inflecting the agenda for change, and New Labour certainly had a keen attentiveness to the importance of the symbolic. This was reflected in early endeavours to introduce a new vocabulary into social work and related spheres. Hence, in terms of children in public care, there was an attempt to promote the 'looked-after' alternative. Connected to this, problematic moves took place to introduce the phrase 'corporate parenting' into local authority initiatives focused on the 'looked after'. During New Labour's first administration – and indicative of the tendency to seek to vapidly 'brand' new programmes – the 'Quality Protects' initiative was launched to try to improve 'outcomes' for this group of children. Similarly, the 'Every Child Matters' slogan was to form the emblematic fulcrum for later programmes. At times, it appeared that Children's Services, increasingly moulded as private sector corporations, were inflating their 'products' and capacity to 'deliver' services that were universally 'excellent' in an uncomplicated world. This approach risked, of course, 'setting social workers up to fail', particularly given that services were often short of staff. Indeed, unfilled vacancies, a high turnover of staff and the dependence on agency staff impacted on the ability of workers within Children's Services throughout the New Labour period. Shortly after the furore surrounding the death of Peter Connelly, it was revealed by the British Association of Social Workers (BASW) that, nationally, about 11% of posts were vacant, rising to 30% in some of the most stressful urban communities ('Social worker chiefs call for end to demonization of their colleagues', *The Guardian*, 13 November 2008, p 15).

New Labour was also intent on direction from the centre and on imposing an audit and 'performance'-based culture throughout all public services. Nevertheless, it appeared to fail to reach its own 'targets', for example, to reduce the numbers of children who were poor. Furthermore, in October 2008, the Audit Commission (2008, p 1) reported that the Children's Trusts created by the government had been 'confused and confusing'. Five years after the publication of *Every child matters* (Chief Secretary to the Treasury, 2003), there was 'little evidence of better outcomes for children and young people' (Audit Commission, 2008, p 1).

More politically, the New Labour approach was heavily influenced by a narrow neoliberal rationality (see Table 1).

Table 1: Seven characteristics of neoliberalisation

Characteristic	Defining feature
Breaking with 'embedded' liberalism	Ceasing to adhere to the social and economic settlement that existed since the Second World War, for example, aiming to achieve full employment and maintaining the welfare state. Injecting market competition into all sectors.
Remaking the state	The state is not 'rolled back', as some argue, but is *reshaped* and *reconfigured* to better serve the demands of capital. This relates to the installation of 'workfare' regimes and how the unemployed, carers and the ill (recoded as 'jobseekers') are cajoled into low-waged employment. Coupled with the evolution of a 'surveillance state'.
Being pragmatic	Refers to the tendency to depart from theoretical purity ('textbook neoliberalism'). In practice, neoliberalism is resilient, has a 'dogged dynamism' and 'fails forward' (Peck, 2010).
Accumulating by dispossessing	Taking from the poor to give to the rich and super-rich.
Injecting precariousness into lives	Often deploying the rhetoric of 'flexibility', injects uncertainty into lives, in and beyond the workplace.
Imprisoning	'Lockdown' is a key feature of neoliberalisation, with the greater use of imprisonment and forms of quasi-confinement for marginalised groups. This process can also be connected to racialisation.
Articulating nationally	Neoliberalism has an affective as well as material dimension. It *looks*, *feels* and *sounds* different in different places (eg Colchester and Cork have branches of MacDonalds seeking to make vast profits but the micro-practices will vary).

Neoliberalism served – often implicitly – to provide the dominant, or hegemonic, core for the 'modernisation' of Children's Services and associated spheres. Some academics and political commentators maintained that New Labour's neoliberalism was 'an uncomfortable and strained construction rather than an essential political character' (Clarke et al, 2007, p 146). However, following Blair's ascendancy to the leadership of the party, it was to become increasingly comfortable with the neoliberal agenda. What Stuart Hall (2003, p 19) referred to as the 'subaltern programme, of a more social-democratic kind, running alongside' became much more subdued, increasingly marginal and marginalised. In a somewhat recalibrated form, neoliberal rationality continues to dominate the perspective of the current Conservative–Liberal Democrat Government.

New Labour was a governing party with a proclivity to look to Washington for direction in shaping policy. Here, Blair was, of course, the most powerful and primary definer. His project to discursively reframe social security benefits as 'handouts' and to incrementally introduce workfare impacted adversely on many of the families engaging with social workers. What remains extraordinary (in England and the Republic of Ireland) is that this inclination to try to replicate approaches from the US is rarely contested within social work's academic literature, despite the fact that the US, one of the most economically unequal societies in the world, hardly represents a successful template for policy relating to children. Figures released by the US government on children (0–17 years) reveal that in 2009, 21% (15.5 million) lived in poverty. This marked an increase from 16% in 2000 and 2001. In 2009, 36% of black children, 33% of Hispanic children and 12% of white, non-Hispanic children lived in poverty. These are increases from 35%, 29% and 10%, respectively, in 2007. Significantly, the percentage of children who lived in families with very high incomes (600% or more of the poverty threshold) nearly doubled, from 7% in 1991 to 13% in 2009 (ChildStats.gov, 2011).

Specifically in terms of social work practice, concerns began to deepen during the New Labour period that social work, as a skill or craft, was being diluted and practitioners were also being distracted from its ethical commitments because of the introduction of e-working. This development has been referred to as the profession's 'e-lectronic turn' (Garrett, 2005) and it was an issue located within a wider public domain following the death of Peter Connelly. The Joint Area Review (JAR) established after Peter's death reported that some cases in Haringey were allocated electronically and without discussion with social workers (Ofsted, Healthcare Commission and HM Inspectorate of Constabulary, 2008). Moreover, a substantial body of research, conducted by Sue White and her colleagues, began to draw attention to the substantial amount of time social workers were compelled to spend in front of computer screens (White et al, 2009).[3]

Ethnographies of social work(ing) over the past 10 years, in and beyond England, have illuminated how practitioners have become disenchanted with their work because it is now characterised by centrally devised assessment schedules, a lack of time, little meaningful contact with the users of services and, more generally, poor working conditions (Jones, 2001; Carey, 2009; White et al, 2009; see also Baines, 2004a, 2004b). Negative developments such as this led to calls within social work's academic literature for a renewed counter-emphasis on the importance of non-directed 'talk' and 'conversation' in social work encounters (see Parton and O'Byrne, 2000). Related to this, Ferguson (2004, p 135) maintained that creativity and 'more soulful forms of work are being suppressed'. These perspectives remain problematic because they are ahistorical and hint at what *real* or *authentic* social work should look and *feel* like. What is more, they remain politically and economically naive for failing to recognise the 'prevailing social order's systematic tendency to create unsatisfying work' (Bellamy Foster, 1998, p ix). Nevertheless, during the finals years of its period in government such critiques were subsumed within New Labour attempts to try to promote alternative *perceptions* of the profession. Once again, political 'spin' was central, as opposed to meaningful change in working practices. Advertisements produced by Publicis, a London advertising agency, for the Children's Workforce Development Unit endeavoured to present social work in a lighter, even gentler, way. The associated 'Be the Difference Campaign' was founded on five adverts, each pivoting on a simple image – a teabag, a piece of plasticine, a doll's house, a crisp, a bouncy ball – and laying the emphasis on the significance of talking with clients. The rhetorical focus was on the

–

possibilities afforded for genuine engagement with the users of services, and on the opportunity for individual workers to be 'the difference'. The emotional tenor, situated in what we can refer to as a new poetics of social work, represented an opportunistic attempt to harness real longing for change within a profession subjected to cuts in services and mundane systems of e-working.

New Labour also tried to reframe practitioner criticisms about the deterioration of working conditions by hinting that such problems could be solved by privatisation, which would create zones of autonomy for professional enrichment and fulfilment. Here, the paradigmatic example was New Labour's promotion of so-called 'social work practices' for 'looked-after' children (Cardy, 2011). Subsequently, while also pressing on with the 'social work practices' plan, David Cameron's administration has trumpeted the idea that working outside the public sector will bring about more fulfilling working lives for practitioners.

More generally, New Labour was to retain a highly ambiguous position in relation to social work. In terms of supporting the profession and its development, a new social work degree was introduced. In addition, the step was taken to introduce a registration system for social work and to make the title 'social worker' protected. Although some commentators worried that this might result in practitioners becoming more subject to surveillance '24/7' (McLaughlin, 2007, 2010), such moves did appear to provide evidence of New Labour's support for the profession. However, at the same time, it seemed to distrust social workers and this dimension was frequently apparent in the inclination to create alternative fields of expertise: for example, personal advisors in the Connexions agency. What is more, policy documents often failed to map, or rendered hazy, a role for social workers within the emerging 'modernisation' agenda.

Even more damagingly, the Blair and Brown administrations failed to adequately defend social workers following the deaths of children in contact with social services departments. There was also a failure to contextualise these deaths by placing them in an international and comparative framework, highlighting that social workers in England appeared to be relatively successful in protecting and safeguarding

–

children. Children in England and Wales are, in fact, less at risk than in most developed countries: the 'baby murder rate is highest in the US and only Greece, Italy, Spain and Sweden have lower rates than England and Wales' ('Urgent inquiry into childcare ordered', *The Guardian*, 13 November 2008, p 14). Moreover, as Polly Toynbee (2008) noted, the numbers of children killed has fallen steadily: down 50% in England and Wales since the 1970s. In the US, as we have seen, so frequently a template for New Labour's 'modernisation' of Children's Services, child murders have risen 17% since the 1970s.

However, the deaths of children cast tragic shadows across the 'reform' programme. Adjo Victoria Climbié, known to child welfare professionals throughout her time in England as Anna Kouao, died in London in February 2000 after suffering neglect and violence from her aunt, Marie Therese Kouao, and her aunt's partner, Carl Manning. In January 2001, they were convicted of the murder of the nine-year-old child and are currently serving sentences of life imprisonment. The Laming Report provided a lengthy, but problematic, exploration of the circumstances surrounding Victoria's death and revealed in stark terms the manifest failure of social work, health and police services to safeguard her and to respond in a competent way to the glaring and multiple concerns about Victoria's welfare during the 11 months that she spent in England (Secretary of State for Health and Secretary of State for the Home Department, 2003). Later that decade, the circumstances surrounding the death of 'Baby P' (later revealed as Peter Connelly) began to dominate political and media discourses on Children's Services. Peter, a 17-month-old boy, died in August 2007 from severe injuries inflicted while he was in the care of his mother, her 'boyfriend' – who was, it appears, 'hidden' from social workers and other professionals – and Jason Owen, a lodger in the household. In November 2008, the two men were found guilty of causing or allowing the death of a child or vulnerable person. The mother had already pleaded guilty to the same charge.

One of the key themes to emerge following these deaths was the vilification of public sector professionals. For example, early in 2008, the Care Standards Tribunal, while deliberating on the case of Victoria's

10

former Haringey social worker, Lisa Arthurworrey, confided that to 'blame everything on Ms. Arthurworrey is … to make her a scapegoat for the failings of a number of people', and casually asserted that there was 'no doubt that Ms. Arthurworrey was seen as *a monster* by many people as a result of Victoria's death' (Care Standards Tribunal, 2008, pp 20, 13, emphasis added). With the case of Peter Connelly, this type of demonisation was once again apparent.

Significantly, New Labour's focal 'modernisation' discourses on children and families were complex because historically rooted ideas continued to impact on policymaking. Blair, for example, seemed to hold a particular vision of child adoption more readily associated with the world of the 1950s than with a world just entering the new millennium. Related to this, an anachronistic evocation of 'problem families' re-emerged as a term within the government's referential frames. Within social work's academic literature, in England, such ideas were echoed in calls for practitioners to exercise 'good authority' over clients who were living in 'poor and disgusting conditions' (Ferguson, 2011, p 97). This notion, coupled with a new interest in the sensory and tactile aspects of practice, hinged on a disavowal of collective solutions to social problems and hinted at a nostalgic hankering for the social work of the 1950s and 1960s, when life seemed simpler and 'problem families' were an easily identifiable target of social opprobrium. Some academics, in their government-commissioned research projects, were also keen to support 'intensive family support projects' (or, as the media preferred, 'sinbins') to curtail the rights and freedoms of poor families (Nixon et al, 2006).

Importantly, this deeply retrogressive dimension to social policy with children and families was reflected in much of the official discourse on 'anti-social behaviour' and – when operating in a more populist vein – 'neighbours from hell'. This tended to incorporate the imagery of the feckless, fecund and troublesome poor who had featured as figures in the discourse of socially retrogressive policymaking for centuries (Pearson, 1975). Shortly after the death of Peter Connelly, for example, *The Observer* argued that the Peter's 'fate' had:

focused the spotlight once again on child protection services and loopholes in the net designed to protect the most vulnerable children, *as well as broader questions of how to reach an underclass of inadequate parents* raising children in volatile circumstances. ('Put more children at risk into care', *The Observer*, 16 November 2008, p 2, emphasis added)

These were, it was asserted, 'families that were straight out of *nightmares* ... an *underclass* ... untouched by the affluence of modern Britain' ('Why children are left to die beyond help's reach', *The Observer*, 16 November 2008, p 18). Here, it could be argued that New Labour's 'ASBO politics' provided the discursive foundation for such press accounts of Peter's death and these 'broader questions'. Moreover, following the death of Peter Connelly, such questions became part of the foundation for the evolution of policies devised by the incoming Conservative–Liberal Democratic Government.

Social work in a 'Big Society': the Conservative–Liberal Democrat administration (2010–present)

For the former Conservative Party leader Iain Duncan Smith, the death of Peter Connelly was a sign of the 'broken society' that he and David Cameron were seeking to fix (see also Blond, 2010). Along with a number of other signatories, he published a letter in *The Guardian* in December 2008 imploring that the Prime Minister seize 'the opportunity of initiating a long-term inquiry to examine how we can stop some of today's children becoming the abusing parents of tomorrow'. This demand for earlier and more substantial interventions into the lives of children and their families was also supported by the then shadow secretary for work and pensions, Chris Grayling, who called for out-of-work parents to have their home lives and prospects investigated in the context of Conservative Party plans to 'tackle underclass Britain' ('"Never-worked" families face Tory scrutiny', *The Observer*, 7 December 2008, p 5). These ideas were later to coalesce around 'troublesome families', who needed to be shepherded into work by so-called 'family champions' (FCs).

The Conservatives' policies amount to a 'cocktail of born-again monetarism and regressive social policies' (Elliott, 2010, p 26). Essentially, at its core, the party remains Thatcherite, but attentive to how their politics are presented and amplified. The tone is much lighter – aching to be 'cool' – and intent on illuminating an inclusive, socially benign deposition. Furthermore, in the context of efforts to detoxify the Conservative 'brand', social work has fulfilled a not inconsequential role. Social work, largely perceived as a liberal profession, constituted one of the groups that the party needed to be seen to re-engage with to convey a more benign image. Just as important, the Conservatives needed to reach into the domain of social work to try to win the votes of disgruntled social work supporters of the embattled Labour Party. Prior to the general election, the party was keen, in fact, to garner the support of the profession (Conservative Party Commission on Social Workers, 2007). On coming to power, the Coalition stated that it would support the 15 recommendations of the Social Work Task Force appointed by the New Labour Government. It also instigated a review of child protection, headed by Eileen Munro, which involved exploring issues related to, for example, early intervention, reducing bureaucracy and providing more professional freedom in order to 'liberate' their skills and talents (Department of Education, 2010). Her final report was published in 2011 and it asserted that there is a pressing 'need to strip away much of the top-down bureaucracy that previous reforms have put in the way of frontline services. Giving professionals greater opportunity for responsible innovation and space for professional judgment is fundamental' (Department of Education, 2011, p 22). Subsequently, the Coalition gave its backing to the setting up of a College of Social Work. In part, therefore, these moves can be perceived as attempts to re-enchant social work, discursively infusing it with a new upbeat 'spirit' in times of austerity (Boltanski and Chiapello, 2005).[4] However, this lighter image of social work appeared especially jarring in early 2012, when the BBC screened three documentaries –

called 'Protecting our children' – which filmed a Bristol social worker visiting a client accompanied by two bulky security guards.

For the Conservatives, the 'broken society' is 'the baleful outcome of social-democratic politics', and the 'source of the corrosion of social life can be found in the excesses of government' (Finlayson, 2010, pp 25–6). This was a theme that was returned to following the summer riots in 2011 (BBC, 2011). Unsurprisingly, given this political perspective, the 'effects of neoliberal competitiveness and inequality are … ignored' (Finlayson, 2010, p 26). For the Coalition, the chief way to respond to the 'broken society' is to dismantle 'the old-fashioned state … the heavy-handed state' and to construct a 'big society' (Cameron, 2010, p 10; see also Norman, 2010). According to Cameron, this 'is about a real cultural shift – we know that the era of big government … didn't work. We want to build a Big Society where local people feel empowered' (Cabinet Office, 2010a, p 1). The Deputy Prime Minister has also placed an emphasis on 'social mobility' (Cabinet Office, 2010b). However, it remains clear that the government is intent on cutting jobs and services within the public sector and that the political aspiration is to usher in 'eternal austerity' and a 'permanently shrunken state' (Toynbee, 2010, p 27). In this context, it will be the very poorest – many of whom are, of course, in contact with social workers – who are likely to suffer the most. This model, as well as representing a threat to the terms and conditions of social workers and embedding discriminatory practices against the poor, heralds not a 'big society', but a 'society characterized by the deliberate dismantling of the social state' (Bourdieu and Wacquant, 2001, p 3).

As with New Labour, the Conservatives remain somewhat ambiguous about the worth of social work. For example, a representative of the current government has gone so far as to state that social work could be undertaken on an entirely voluntary basis by 'retired City bankers or ex-insurance brokers' ('Minister calls for more child protection volunteers', *The Guardian*, 30 October 2010, p 21; see also Department of Education, 2010, p 2). In terms of social work with children and families, developments on the margins of mainstream practice are also likely to be significant. Here, the appearance of FCs is important in three senses. First, it hints at aspirations to create an alternative way of intervening in the lives of children and families, providing a type of 'social work' that is cheap, even nil cost. Second, it seeks to annex interventions in the lives of children and families to one that is central – getting people into low-waged work. Finally, it contains within it key ideas about 'clients' that seek to infantilise them.

Lying outside of social work organisational structures, FCs focus on 'troublesome families', who are framed as idle work units in need of 'support' so as to prompt their entry into work (Family Champion Employment Guide, 2007). This form of intervention is infused with an affective vibe, 'positive psychology' and 'can-do' ambiance, but the determining orientation remains palpably neoliberal and punitive (Family Champion Employment Guide, 2007). In the Foreword to this guide, it is maintained that the FC 'vision [is] to help 100,000 families to become working families, paying their own way, living great lives and what's more, helping others do the same'. Individual FCs must, therefore, 'inspire and change attitudes; to make sure every bit of the existing government, voluntary and private effort adds up to this single goal of creating happy, working families'. The training document insists that an FC needs to 'make *your* family want to work' (Family Champion Employment Guide, 2007, emphasis added). Grounded in the belief that individuals are at fault and paying no heed to the lack of jobs and structural issues, the aim is to 'build their self esteem and make them feel that employment is achievable, and not a pipedream'. When 'looking for a job' it is necessary, therefore, to consider working for an employer, yet not receiving any pay.

The FC literature is predicated on the idea that people *must* enter the capitalist labour market. Hence, the emphasis is on how potential workers should present themselves to employers and bodily convey how they have inculcated appropriate demeanours:

> Both the applicant and their clothes must be clean. There is no excuse for poor hygiene. Ensure that your family member is aware that they must have a bath or a shower on the day of the interview, they must use a deodorant and they must brush

their teeth. Get them to check clothes for stray hair and remove any found. Get them to iron their clothes. (Family Champion Employment Guide, 2007)

FCs are not social workers and drawing attention to such developments is not meant to suggest that social workers are keen to be incorporated within workfare regimes. However, despite the common image of the profession as left-leaning, there is some evidence to suggest that practitioners are not averse to harsher treatment being dealt to the unemployed. For example, in 2007, when New Labour proposed restricting income support for parents appearing not to be 'seeking work' once their children reached age 12, rather than 16, 80% of respondents to a *Community Care* poll – not all, of course, likely to be social workers, and neither can this poll be regarded as 'scientific' – agreed with this proposal, expressing the view that lone parents should be encouraged to go back to work (Brody, 2007).

How, therefore, can social work with children and families in the Republic of Ireland be assessed in the current period? The contemporary academic literature in the Republic of Ireland tends to be rather narrow in its focus and fails to incorporate a more expansive and political reading of social work. However, two key factors are presently shaping the trajectory of social work: the economic crisis, the impact of which is even more severe than in England; and the publication of inquiries on child abuse in the past.

The Republic of Ireland

Economic meltdown: social work and the dismantling of the social state

From the advent of the partially independent state in 1922, elite groups were hesitant to embrace social work because it was viewed, especially by senior figures within the Roman Catholic Church, as a harbinger of modernity. Perhaps more specifically, they were fearful of what they saw as its potential ability to intervene in the 'private' sphere of family life (Skehill, 2004; Kearney and Skehill, 2005). As the influential John Charles McQuaid (1895–1973), the Catholic Archbishop of Dublin and Primate of Ireland (1940–73), stated in the early 1950s: 'Our people do not want lady analysts of their lives and motives. Trouble is certain to develop if almoners undertake psychological investigation in our homes and hospitals' (quoted in Skehill, 2004, p 163). Perhaps, also, the idea persisted that social work was a 'Protestant' endeavour and, as such, it was – as McQuaid's remarks suggest – contrary to the 'Catholic' ethos of the inchoate state. In time, however, such concerns diminished, but the specific role accorded to the family – recognised in the Irish Constitution, *Bunreacht Eireann*, in 1937 – has continued, some argue, to place limitations on how social workers and the courts can intervene in this 'private sphere' to safeguard the rights of children. Many are of the view that an amendment to the constitution, which was the focus of a referendum in 2012, will counteract this perceived bias.

Social work with children and families is now broadly similar to social work activity in England and practitioners share many of the same professional concerns (Burns and Lynch, 2008). For example, many are critical that the changing nature of the 'work' in social work: recent research has revealed practitioners' concern about the eroding of the opportunity to make relationships with the users of services that can 'make a difference' (Burns, 2008, p 67). Organisationally, within the state sector, social work is administratively situated within the HSE, which is the biggest employer of social workers, with just under 60% of all posts and some 72% of newly qualified social workers going on to work for it (NSWQB, 2006, p 26).[5] Importantly also, the social work workforce is very clearly a multinational labour force: 32.7% have non-national social work qualifications (NSWQB, 2006, p 29); in addition, 5.7% of social workers have qualified across the border in Northern Ireland (see also Walsh et al, 2010). As a profession, social work is somewhat more functional and less associated with ideas connected to emancipatory practice than, for example, social work in England. Indeed, it has been noted that 'little evidence exists of practices or policies in social work to accommodate increased diversity' (Walsh et al, 2010, p 7). As Trish Walsh and her colleagues maintain:

[T]he development of specific texts on working with refugees and asylum seekers and the inclusion of equality and human rights on social work courses have not translated into visible anti-racist or anti-oppressive policies or practices in social work … in many cases, even an appropriate sensitivity to the needs of those not considered fully Irish…. The lack of attention to cultural differences in child protection guidelines and child welfare legislation is one tangible example of a continuing inertia. (Walsh et al, 2010, p 7)

Historically, the state in the Republic has been consistently neglectful towards economically and socially marginalised children and families. Even at the peak of the boom and during the years of corporate 'partnership' – which brought together government ministers, business leaders and the higher echelons of the trade union bureaucracy – the Republic:

had little reason to boast about its social performance. It ranked second-to-bottom in the OECD [Organisation for Economic Co-operation and Development] league tables for poverty and inequality; only the US fared worse. Inequality increased during the period of highest economic growth, with the number of households earning below 50 per cent of the average income rising from 18 per cent in 1994 to 24 per cent in 2001. Other benchmarks shifted in the opposite direction: government expenditure on social protection as a proportion of GDP [Gross Domestic Product] stood at 20 per cent in 1993, but had fallen to 14 per cent by 2000 – barely half the EU's average. (Finn, 2011, p 12)

Clearly, the economic crisis that has engulfed the Republic is inseparable from a wider international crisis. Ireland was the first country in the eurozone to adopt a neoliberal-infused 'austerity' budget. In late 2010, as the crisis deepened, the International Monetary Fund (IMF) and European Central Bank (ECB) provided a 'bailout' package that resulted in further punitive public spending cuts and a dilution – some would argue, eradication – of national sovereignty. Social workers, along with other public sector workers, have experienced massive cuts in pay. A budget in December 2010, the fourth in little over two years, cut even deeper into public spending (Barnardos, 2010). Following 'austerity' budgets, the 'total fiscal tightening up' now stands at 'nearly 20% of GDP, more than double the Tory-led Coalition cuts in Britain' (Burke, 2011, p 140). What is more, in a stark 'reprise of the colonial relationship ... the major holder of Irish government debt are the British banks, with state-owned Royal Bank of Scotland at the front of the queue' (Burke, 2011: 141).

After the general election in February 2011, a government headed by Fine Gael, with the Labour Party as coalition partner, was formed but there is no indication that the crisis is to end or that this administration is intent on embarking on a new, more socially and economically benign, course. Furthermore, it would be entirely erroneous to assume that the ECB and IMF have 'pushed the Dublin government down a path it would rather not tread', given that 'their suggestions have been accepted with something that closely resembles glee' (Finn, 2011, p 13). Economic elites have been keen to 'take on' the public sector unions for some years and are now using the crisis to pursue a ruthless form of class politics (see also Klein, 2007). Unsurprisingly, therefore, the 'emigrant boat and plane have re-emerged' as social safety valves: the number of people leaving the state rising by one quarter between 2006 and 2008 ('Emigration must be confronted', *The Irish Times*, 23 September 2010).

Looking to the past for messages about the present: the Ryan Report and the contemporary crisis in safeguarding children

In the early years of the 21st century, discussion on child abuse has mostly focused on that perpetrated by priests and members of religious orders (Murphy et al, 2005; Commission of Investigation, 2009, 2010; Commission to Inquire into Child Abuse, 2009). In what follows, the focus will be on one of these inquiries: the voluminous and distressing

Commission to Inquire into Child Abuse – henceforth, the Ryan Report – which reported on abuse in Industrial Schools and related institutions. It is significant not only because of what it tells us about state responses to children and families in the past, but because it provides a optic through which contemporary ways of relating to children and families, by social workers and other professions, can be assessed and weighted.

Industrial Schools were established by legislation, enacted in 1868, to hold and contain neglected, abandoned and ambiguously 'troublesome' children. Despite being a measure introduced by the British administration, following partial independence in 1922, these institutions expanded: between 1936 and 1970, 170,000 children were committed to Industrial Schools, for an average seven-year stay.

The Ryan Commission heard evidence from 1,090 men and women. In terms of the specific types of abuse suffered, more than 90% reported being physically abused while in the Industrial Schools or out-of-home care. They:

> frequently described casual, random physical abuse but many wished to report only the times when the frequency and severity were such that they were injured or in fear for their lives. In addition to being hit and beaten, witnesses described other forms of abuse such as being flogged, kicked and otherwise physically assaulted, scalded, burned and held under water. (Ryan Report, Executive Summary, p 13)

Absconders, colloquially referred to as 'runners', were 'severely beaten, at times publicly. Some had their heads shaved and were humiliated' (Ryan Report, Executive Summary, p 20).

Although no definitive evidence exists relating to the operation of organised 'rings' of abusers, sexual abuse was reported by approximately half of all the witnesses appearing before Ryan's Confidential Committee: 'Acute and chronic contact and non-contact sexual abuse was reported, including vaginal and anal rape, molestation and voyeurism in both isolated assaults and on a regular basis over long periods of time' (Ryan Report, Executive Summary, p 13). Sexual abuse was:

> endemic in boys' institutions [which comprised the majority]. The situation in girls' institutions was different. Although girls were subjected to predatory sexual abuse by male employees or visitors or in outside placements, sexual abuse was not systemic in girls' schools. (Ryan Report, Executive Summary, p 21)

Detainees were also victims of neglect and emotional abuse. This was:

> reported by witnesses in the form of lack of attachment and affection, loss of identity, deprivation of family contact, humiliation, constant criticism, personal denigration, exposure to fear and the threat of harm.... Witnesses were incorrectly told their parents were dead and were given false information about their siblings and family members. (Ryan Report, Executive Summary, p 13)

Given the scope of this abuse, it is hardly surprising that many witnesses had to deal with its impact throughout their lives:

> Witnesses ... described lives marked by poverty, social isolation, alcoholism, mental illness, sleep disturbance, aggressive behaviour and self harm. Approximately 30% of the witnesses described a constellation of ongoing, debilitating mental health concerns for example; suicidal behaviour, depression, alcohol and substance abuse and eating disorders, which required treatment including psychiatric admission, medication and counselling. (Ryan Report, Executive Summary, p 14)

Significantly, there was a constant flow of knowledge about what was occurring within the Industrial Schools, although this was apt to be disregarded by the state and the evidence of brave and vocal survivors of the system was suppressed (see Tyrrell, 2006). This was because those who 'spoke out' tended be marginalised and lacked the power to define and name abusive practices within the wider public domain. There were great difficulties presented for dissenting and oppositional voices because of the power of the Roman Catholic Church and the social standing and status of priests, nuns and other associated religious figures. Related to this, state 'officials often labelled those who broke this silence as cranks and troublemakers' (Holohan, 2011, p 147).

Poverty was a vital and pivotal factor leading to the incarceration of children in Industrial Schools. In official circles, such poor families were regarded with contempt, and from the early years of the new state, only established in 1922, the 'impoverished child was viewed as a burden' (Holohan, 2011, p 188) and perceived as 'other', potentially contaminating the hegemonic Irish Republican ideal of petty bourgeois civility and propriety. Witnesses reported:

> being subjected to ridicule about their parents and families, most often in public, in the course of being abused. The sons of lone mothers, 'orphans' or 'conventers' were reported as particular targets for such abuse, being told that their mothers were 'sinners', 'slags' and 'old whores' who did not want them or could not care for them. Others reported hearing their families described as 'scum', 'tramps' and 'from the gutter'. Witnesses admitted to institutions in the context of family difficulties reported being subjected to the constant denigration of their parents. Witnesses recalled being constantly told their parents were 'alcoholics', 'prostitutes', 'mad' and 'no good'. (Ryan Report, vol 3, p 107)

More generally, the position of the Roman Catholic Church within the Republic is historically significant because it was 'primarily governance from the Church rather than the state which framed interventions with children and families' (Skehill, 2004, pp 52–3). As a later report into child abuse in the Archdiocese of Dublin observed, the Church not only remains 'a religious organisation', but continues to be 'a human/ civil instrument of control and power' (Commission of Investigation, 2009, p 14). Despite never being an omnipotent presence, the Church has undoubtedly been a key component in the hegemonic ensemble responsible for governing Irish society.

The Church also remains a significant ideological and material power within the Republic. Its power may be 'slowly and subtly eroding, but it is still strong. No one is afraid of priests anymore ... but they still appoint the teachers and run the schools' (Toibin, 2005, p 6). For example, although the new government appears to be committed to changing the situation, the Church currently 'controls 2,899 of the 3,282 primary schools in the state, catering for 92 per cent of pupils' (O'Toole, 2009, p 3). What this underlines is the 'vulnerability of a State which owns and controls so little of its vital social infrastructure' (Raftery, 2009, p 16). The Church has also been historically resistant to child-centred education and frequently stymied the development of public health systems.

In contemporary Ireland, it is clear that the treatment of young prisoners continues to replicate that of the detainees in Industrial Schools. According to Irish prison chaplains, the way that young prisoners – those aged 16 to 21 – are 'managed' in the much-criticised St. Patrick's Institution raises particular concerns. This is the largest facility in the state for young offenders, and national and international bodies have repeatedly condemned the deplorable conditions there over the past 25 years. Those 'young people detained in St Patrick's Institution are [like inmates of Industrial Schools in the past] not allowed to wear their own clothes (unlike every other prisoner in every other prison)' (Irish Prison Chaplains, 2010, p 19). As the chaplains summarise, St Patrick's Institution 'is a "warehouse" for young people.... It is a demoralising, destructive and dehumanising experience, with few redeeming features' (Irish Prison Chaplains, 2010, p 20).

Similarly, asylum seekers are rigidly segregated, with 52 direct provision centres established in April 2000 and almost 6,000 asylum seekers still living in them for more than three years. These are privately operated establishments with contracts with the Reception and Integration Agency (RIA): residents are given €19.10 each week to live on and provided with a shared room and meals in 'hotel-style' accommodation. A person waiting for their asylum claim to be decided by the state has no right to work. Even more seriously, many unaccompanied children seeking asylum went missing from state care in the past decade. Importantly also, a 2004 amendment to the constitution provided that children born on the island of Ireland to parents who were both non-nationals would no longer have an automatic and constitutional right to Irish citizenship.

Continuing anxieties also exist about the practice of placing children in adult psychiatric wards. At least 100 children under the age of 18 were admitted to adult psychiatric facilities in 2010 despite a commitment by the HSE to phase out the practice. An inspector of mental health services has 'described the practice of admitting children to adult centres as "inexcusable, counter-therapeutic and almost custodial" in that clinical supervision is provided by teams unqualified in child and adolescent psychiatry' ('100 children placed in adult psychiatric units', *The Irish Times*, 7 October 2010, p 2; see also Bonnar, 2010).

The Health and Information and Quality Authority (HIQA) has also reported that staff in one third of the state's residential centres had not been properly vetted and the children placed there were at unnecessary risk. Similarly, many foster carers have not been vetted. HIQA has also called on the HSE to immediately cease using one of its three secure units for troubled and vulnerable young people – Ballydowd – due to concerns over the safety of child residents. This was echoed by HIQA in subsequent reports, which expressed 'grave concerns regarding the safety for children' within one of the other units, Coovagh House in Limerick (HIQA, 2010a, 2010b, 2010c).

During 2010, the deaths of children and young people 'in care' and the failure of the HSE to produce robust and reliable data emerged as a key issue. In March 2010, it was reported that the HSE had not published a single report on the death of a child in state care since it was formed in 2005. Moreover, no independent child death review system was in place until that same month, when the Minister for Children established an expert group to investigate the deaths of children in 'care' over the last decade. Revealing the inadequacy of information retrieval systems across the HSE, which had not been satisfactorily addressed during the so-called 'Celtic Tiger' period, a senior manager in the agency stated that assembling numbers on the deaths of children was difficult because it involved checking manual records and relying on the local knowledge of social workers ('HSE to give number of child deaths in state care', *The Irish Times*, 28 May 2010, p 7). It was later announced that at least 188 young people who were in care or in contact with social services have died over the past decade. However, an HSE official said that the number could rise further still if social work teams around the country found evidence of further deaths ('Child deaths in care or in contact with services now at 188', *The Irish Times*, 5 June 2010, p 1). In December 2010, it was revealed that the number of children who had died had risen to 199, 11 more than was announced by the HSE in June ('HSE revises figures for deaths of children', *The Irish Times*, 9 December 2010, p 3). This figure was subsequently revised downwards – to 196 – by an Independent Child Death Review Group in June 2012 (Shannon and Gibbons, 2012).

Reflecting the state's incompetence, and also its brazen cynicism in censoring troublesome accounts of how children are not safeguarded, a report on the deaths of children in Monageer, in Wexford, was drastically redacted and a number of pages – bizarrely including many of the report's recommendations – were deleted (Lunny et al, 2008). The names of key officials connected to children who either died or were abused in public care are routinely omitted from subsequently published inquiry reports (see, eg, Report of a Committee of Inquiry, 1996; Gibbons, 2010). The 'awareness' and 'consistent implementation' of *Children first* (Department of Health and Children, 1999) – the protocol guiding arrangements for inter-professional working and the protection and welfare of children – remains 'a continuing challenge' (Office of the Minister for Children and Youth Affairs, 2008, p v). In this context, two key issues are significant:

> the absence of consistency in the delivery of child welfare and protection services across the country and, more importantly, the absence of any standards against which delivery of services

> can be benchmarked and monitored.... [It is] incontrovertible
> that there are major inconsistencies in the implementation of
> the 'Children First' guidelines throughout the country. (Office
> of the Minister for Children and Youth Affairs, 2008, pp 14–15)

Kemp (2008, p 107) has detected a somewhat paradoxical tendency in
that the 'more attempts are made to control and standardize practice,
the more divergent practice appears to have become'. Specifically in
terms of *Children first*, no 'sooner had the document been launched than
variations were adopted by each Health Board. Instead of standardising
practice, it merely led to greater degrees of divergence and localised
arrangements' (Kemp, 2008, p 107). The current government is to
place *Children first* on a statutory footing. More controversially, under
a measure contained in the Criminal Justice Withholding Information
on Crimes and against Children and Vulnerable Persons Bill, it is to
become mandatory for organisations and individuals to report instances
of possible child abuse. The Coalition administration is also intent on
establishing a new Child and Family Support Agency (CFSA), which
will be separate from the HSE. It is likely to be established in 2013.

As the earlier discussion on England suggests, the Republic is not the
only European state encountering difficulties in maintaining a robust
system of child welfare and child protection, but the way in which
the problem is emerging is clearly nationally specific and needs to be
located conjuncturally and in relation to other developments within
the troubled jurisdiction. The dominant 'official' narrative maintains
that a measure of 'reform' is urgently required. Often, such ideas are
heavily influenced by 'reforms' introduced in England during the
New Labour period: for example, the *Every child matters* agenda (Chief
Secretary to the Treasury, 2003) and the notion that child welfare
services can be 'transformed' by new systems of e-working (which, as
we saw, have been largely discredited). There is also a tendency to echo
keywords derived from the discourse of 'reform' across the Irish Sea
(see also Williams, 1983): for example, it has been argued that pressures
experienced by the HSE 'could be addressed through *partnerships*

with all us concerned with children and families' (Dolan, 2010, p 16, emphasis added; see also Table 2).

Table 2: Cutting and pasting from New Labour

Every child matters (Chief Secretary to the Treasury, 2003)	The 'vision for a quality Irish childhood' (Task Force on the Child and Family Support Agency, 2012)
To stay safe	To be safe from accidental and intentional harm/Secure in the immediate and wider physical environment
To make a positive contribution	To be part of positive networks of family, friends, neighbours and the community/Included and participating in society
To achieve economic well-being	To be economically secure
To be healthy	To be healthy, both physically and mentally
To enjoy and achieve	To be supported in active learning

Clearly, attempts to 'reform' a ramshackle and chaotic system of child welfare and child protection may impact in favourable ways. However, these approaches are largely inadequate because they fail to recognise how the state has functioned in the Republic of Ireland. To better understand the evident and serious problems, it is vital to analyse historical and contemporary state practices and the patterning of economic and social relations within Ireland. More fundamentally, it will be impossible to truly reform the dysfunctional system without an extensive and embracing political project of state transformation.

Conclusion: a child protection economy and the new radical social work

The beginning of the global economic crisis represented what historian Eric Hobsbawm (2008, p 28) termed the 'most serious crisis of the capitalist system since 1929–33'. In September 2008, when the financial crisis seemed to deepen – as stock markets around the world began to falter and plummet and a number of banking, mortgage and insurance companies failed – the US administration was prompted to intervene decisively and to pass the Emergency Economic Stabilization Act 2008: a measure that provided for greater government intervention and that seemed to run entirely counter to the rhetoric of neoliberalism.

Indeed, these emergency measures, introduced in North America, Europe and elsewhere, appeared to indicate something of a Keynesian resurgence. Subsequent 'quantitative easing' measures – governments propping up the failing economic system by injecting huge amounts of money – have been introduced in all the major Western economies. However, the 'price to be paid' for such initiatives will be met, according to the dominant neoliberal rationality, by the working class and the unemployed poor, who form the core group involved with social work services, particularly those engaging with children and families.

It remains apparent that the neoliberal project, which many thought had come to a conclusion with the 'crash', has, in fact, been emboldened and the unfolding and unresolved economic crisis is now being utilised to *reinforce* economic cleavages and deepen class inequalities. In this sense, the relatively small economy of Greece is being used as a 'laboratory' to try and ascertain how far neoliberalisation can be pushed. However, in the Republic of Ireland also, it is the poorest that are facing the most severe cuts: 16.3% of children in Ireland live in poverty, well above the OECD average of 12.7% ('More Irish children live in poverty than OECD average', *The Irish Times*, 19 April 2011, p 3). Despite this, punitive budget cuts in 2009 represented a €31 drop in the weekly household budget for a family of four wholly reliant on social welfare. In the same budget, a lone parent with two children became poorer by €21.52 every week (Barnardos, 2010). Across the globe, it is also clear that a redistribution to the rich is taking place during a period of so-called 'austerity', when, in the words of the UK Prime Minister, we are allegedly 'all in this together' (Cameron, 2010). The world's 'high net worth individuals' (HNWIs) 'expanded in population and wealth in 2010 surpassing 2007 pre-crisis levels in nearly every region'. Moreover, the 'global population of Ultra-HNWIs grew by 10.2% in 2010 and its wealth by 11.5%' (Merrill Lynch and Capgemini, 2011).

What, therefore, is to be done? Having briefly surveyed the present situation in England and the Republic of Ireland, it is apparent that the various strategies to introduce 'reforms' into the area of Children's Services are unlikely to succeed. For example, the vote in the Republic of Ireland to alter the constitution to incorporate an attentive to the paramountcy of the child's welfare is unlikely to genuinely transform the lives of children: if a child with special needs has lost a teacher because of budget cuts, having recourse to the constitution will not alter the situation, only a qualitatively different set of political and economic priorities will be beneficial to the child. Similarly, the introduction of 'magic bullet' measures, such as the mandatory reporting of child abuse or the creation of the CFSA, is unlikely to prove worthwhile in the long term. What is required is not a reshaped child protection *system*, but a child protection *economy* that serves and safeguards all children.

In this context, therefore, it remains important to understand that those seeking to promote neoliberal approaches are intent on a 'long war' and on ensuring that change takes place and becomes embedded over many years, even decades. Given this project, there is a need to create a different set of social and political possibilities founded on total opposition to a destabilised and vengeful capitalism. Here, the challenge is to create a European movement intent on building new alliances and to participate in actions that are intent on resisting capital's endeavour to remake and reorder the world. Specifically, in terms of social work, engaging in such oppositional activity is, of course, a far from easy task because those in positions of structural power (and invested with the power of naming and defining) seek to maintain hegemony and identify what is permissible and what should be 'closed down'. Within academic institutions, educators are often constrained because programmes have curricula that are predetermined and mapped out by central 'authorities' and 'experts'. This is not to argue that there are no 'spaces' for a more critical engagement within social work education and practice. Indeed, the growth of the Social Work Action Network (SWAN) hints at the possibilities for a new radical social work (Lavalette, 2011b). This initiative might help us to remember that another social work is possible.

Notes

[1] Policy on Children's Services in Scotland, Wales and Northern Ireland, although frequently dominated discursively by the same preoccupations, has not always mirrored that in England. I ceased to practise as a social worker in the late 1990s when I became a full-time academic. I mention this not in an apologetic way or to highlight a deficit in what follows, but merely to remind readers, because there may be an embedded tendency for writers, working as full-time academics and teaching social work, to neglect the fact that their being located beyond the field of practice impacts on their perspective. Being a social work academic may confer certain advantages – for example, in enabling a more panoramic view of the state of play – but there are inescapable disadvantages in being beyond the everyday world of social work.

[2] Antonio Gramsci (22 January 1891–27 April 1937) was an Italian writer, Marxist politician and theorist. A founding member and leading member of the Communist Party of Italy, he was imprisoned by Mussolini's fascist regime. At his trial, Gramsci's prosecutor famously stated: 'For 20 years we must stop this brain from functioning'. However, during his period in prison (1927–37), he completed more than 30 notebooks and 3,000 pages of history and analysis, which continue to furnish an important resource for those trying to understand the resilient and fluid nature of capitalist hegemony.

[3] One of the foremost symbols of the New Labour period was the laptop computer, and dataveillance was to play an increasingly prominent role. The planned Contactpoint database on children was to prove especially controversial on account of its Orwellian conception. Unsurprisingly, such moves resulted in concerns about what social theorists have termed the 'surveillance society'. Critics of the Contactpoint plan were also fearful that the information located on this mooted national database was unlikely to be secure.

[4] What follows draws on Garrett (2012a).

[5] The HSE is a quasi-governmental organisation that operates at arm's-length from the elected government and minister with responsibility

for health and related services. The current government has stated that it is to abolish the HSE. The setting up of such an agency is a typical neoliberal measure that serves to dilute democratic accountability while also facilitating further privatisation. In August 2010, the Social Work Registration Board was set up. This is influenced by developments in the UK mentioned earlier. Many social workers have refused to register because the cost of registration is regarded as amounting to yet another significant pay cut.

The crisis in social work with children and families: response to Paul Michael Garrett

Rona Woodward

Introduction

Paul Michael Garrett offers a powerful indictment of state and Church responses to children and young people in the Republic of Ireland. He also argues persuasively against the 'spirit of reform' that characterised New Labour's approach to social work in the UK and is now embraced equally enthusiastically by the Conservative–Liberal Democrat Coalition. Garrett emphasises the relentless nature of the neoliberal advance and the extent to which it has already 'remade' society. He is clear about the damage done to social work with children and families (to both workers and service users) and recognises that the onslaught is far from over. Although there is nothing in Paul's article that I disagree with, I would like to raise additional points about poverty, inequality and injustice in relation to children and families policy and practice because, as austerity gains a stronghold across the UK, it is those who are already disadvantaged who stand to lose most. There are oppositional voices in social work – Garrett mentions the Social Work Action Network (www.socialworkfuture. org), an organisation uniting practitioners, academics, service users and students in campaigning for social work as social justice. Social work, however, is often both 'oppressive and conservative' (Weiss-Gal et al, 2012) and, for many working-class families especially, it can feel like

—

little more than surveillance and control (Jones, 2009). Where relevant, I want to include a Scottish perspective. Scotland has its own parliament and may yet vote for independence, but how far does the language of 'social justice' and 'solidarity' (Mooney and Scott, 2012) take us down the road of genuine improvements for children and families?

The poverty problem

The detrimental effects of poverty on children and families are widely recognised. Poverty means much more than low income; it is associated with personal, social and environmental deprivation and high levels of fear, victimisation and stress, as well as stigma and unequal rights (see, eg, Tomlinson and Walker, 2009; McKendrick et al, 2011). Poverty in Scotland increased dramatically during the Conservative Party's first neoliberal campaign (1979 to 1997), as it did across the UK. Child poverty in the UK then decreased slowly in places between 1997 and 2006 under New Labour's tax and benefit reforms (Hills and Stewart, 2005), and figures suggest that, at this time, Scotland actually did better than England in terms of child poverty due to the effective interplay between reserved and devolved powers (Hothersall and Walker, 2010; JRF, 2010). However, as in England, there was no Scottish improvement in terms of social and economic inequality, as the gulf between the rich and poor widened, and poverty itself remained widespread (Mooney, 2011). Although poverty is better understood across the UK and attracts more policy attention as a result, there is still little hope for people living in 'entrenched poverty' and in areas experiencing 'long-term economic decline' (Batty et al, 2011, p 39).

The policy problem

A new Child Poverty Act was introduced in 2010, setting targets for the eradication of child poverty in the UK. As a result, both the Scottish Nationalist Government and the Conservative-led Coalition in London now have their own anti-poverty strategies for children (DfE, 2011; Scottish Government, 2011). These developments offer fine examples of policy contradiction, however, given the extent to which recession and the related austerity programme have widened the economic gulf between rich and poor and between young and old (Leach and Hanton, 2012). 'Tackling' child poverty remains at the centre of the policy agenda, however. The London-based Coalition neatly sums up the 'causes' of poverty as 'worklessness', 'debt', 'educational failure' and 'family and relationship breakdown', all washed down with a healthy measure of New Labour policy failure (DfE, 2011, pp 8–20). Unsurprisingly, at no point does the Coalition acknowledge that unequal access to economic and social resources is fundamental to capitalist modes of governance and instrumental in keeping some rich and some poor. The Scottish policy agenda makes more sense of the structural roots of poverty and inequality – with a recognition of 'underlying social and economic determinants of poverty' (Scottish Government, 2011, p 2) – but the Scottish National Party (SNP) also looks for answers at individual and community rather than societal levels. For example, like its Conservative–Liberal Democrat counterpart, the SNP remains wedded to the idea that work remains the main route out of poverty (Mooney, 2011).

In Scotland, in an attempt to be more socially progressive than London and bypass the 'Big Society' agenda (Bone, 2012), there is also a focus on prevention and early intervention to tackle poverty, maximising household resources and strengthening support for children in their early years. Social workers have long had an income-maximisation role (although welfare rights advice has been lost to social work in some local authorities as services have become increasingly specialised and fragmented), but, arguably, there is now little point in focusing social work energies on income maximisation; recent changes to the tax and benefit system have left us with little income to maximise! One would think that social workers could easily assume a key role in early intervention, but, again, this is not without difficulty. Although public services are not as yet retreating in Scotland in the same way as in England (for analysis across public service provision, see Mooney and Scott, 2012), it has recently been argued that the early intervention agenda underpinning all social policy for children in Scotland (eg 'Getting it Right for Every Child' [GIRFEC] and *The early years framework*, as well as the anti-poverty initiative) prioritises universal services and effectively 'locks out' children and families social workers from early intervention (McGhee and Waterhouse, 2011). Thus, children and families social workers are 'locked into' work with those at highest risk, reinforcing 'detection and identification of children at risk of abuse and neglect [and] maintaining high levels of referral to the child protection and hearings systems'[1] (McGhee and Waterhouse, 2011, p 6).

Social policy for children and families in England emphasises, as Garrett argues, enduring political assumptions about individuals failing to take responsibility, and about work being the route out of poverty ('happy working families'). He has a bit of a laugh with Westminster's 'family champion' model but is clear that the underlying sentiment is divisive – a veiled attack on poor families. Similarly, despite a nod to universal services, the anti-poverty initiative in England outlines 'targeted support' for disadvantaged children and families and 'intensive support' for families with 'multiple problems' (DfE, 2011), again turning the spotlight on poor and disadvantaged children, families and neighbourhoods. The same can be said for the Coalition's recent 'Troubled Families' initiative, designed to deal with the 'problem' of '120,000 never-worked' families. The 'Troubled Families' 'expert', Louise Casey, spoke to 16 out of 120,000 families with multiple problems (with no discussion about how the figure of 120,000 was reached in the first place!) and found that:

> Listening to the families there was a strong sense of them having problems and causing problems for years.... In many cases their problems began with their own parents and their parents' parents, in cycles of childhood abuse, violence and care which are then replayed in their own lives. (Casey, 2012, p 3)

Casey repeats powerful assumptions about the nature of social problems: that particular families cause trouble for themselves, their children, their communities and wider society. Her report adopts an understanding tone but still demonises *troubled families* because they: have many children; maintain dysfunctional, violent relationships and networks; abuse their children physically and sexually; rely on social services and state care; are teenage mothers; fail to keep their children in school; experience mental ill health; and misuse substances. Scottish policy at least makes the link between the difficulties families face and the poverty and deprivation they experience, but Casey's take on *troubled families* reinforces every stereotype available. For example, research evidence about child abuse is sidestepped, in particular, that it takes many forms and occurs in all socio-economic groups. While poverty is associated with child neglect in particular, poverty does *not* cause child abuse (see NSPCC, 2008; Daniel et al, 2012). The evidence about teenage parents is also ignored, although it indicates that teenage parenting does *not* mean that both mothers and children fare badly (Duncan, 2007). Casey suggests that family intervention workers (the social work role is unclear) must concentrate on 'lay[ing] bare the extent of the dysfunction' in *troubled families* (Casey, 2012, p 64). Just how does one 'lay bare dysfunction'? Is *all* the money to go on the 24/7 'social working' of 120,000 *troubled families*? If so, what about other children and families in need?

The practice problem

Much has been written about the neoliberal programme to strengthen market capitalism (Harvey, 2005) and its damaging effect on society (Wilkinson and Pickett, 2010; Dorling and Thomas, 2011) and social work (Harris, 2003; Ferguson and Woodward, 2009). As Paul argues both in his lead article and elsewhere (Garrett, 2003, 2009), social work with children and families is particularly vulnerable to external and internal attempts to 'transform' and 'modernise'. The neoliberal change agenda promotes rationing of resources, bureaucratisation, individualisation and de-professionalisation (Rogowski, 2012a). Social workers often lack support and supervision while working under intolerable pressure (Penketh, 2009), while service users face tighter eligibility criteria, fewer public services, privatisation and profiteering at their expense, and diminishing income and life chances (Bone, 2012). For Williams (2011, p 73, emphasis in original): 'Social workers are on the front line of the neoliberal deception both by being *acted on* by the neoliberal modernizing project but also as *agents of it*. The professional agenda has been ideologically controlled and its critique muted.'

It would be disingenuous to suggest that the problems facing social work with children and families stem solely from 30 years of neoliberal reform, however. Historically, any critique that social work offered was 'muted'. I agree with Paul when he argues that social work cannot be viewed as 'benign' and 'emancipatory' and I emphasise earlier that for some working-class children and families, social work is simply social control. It is worrying, therefore, that policy moves across the UK, alhough, arguably, less destructively in Scotland than in England, are pushing social workers closer to risk management, surveillance and control. This is not to suggest that social work with children and families should avoid all aspects of social control. Where families are struggling and children are in need, there is a role for health and social care professionals. There is still debate to be had, however, about what that role should be and with whom. Like Paul, I fear for our current child welfare system, with its emphasis on risk, crisis and control in respect of working-class families. Theoretically and experientially, we know that child abuse and neglect are cross-class occurrences, yet we still struggle to identify children who are at risk but who do not fall within our traditional working-class focus (Jones, 2009; Daniel et al, 2012).

Social work has yet to decide what it is and where it is going. It has always been reluctant (at best!) to commit to radical[2] ideas, but inbuilt conservativism cannot fully explain why the profession remains bogged down in where it has been. Social work continues to rely on traditional approaches to education and practice that sideline the structural nature of many individual problems (Mackay and Woodward, 2010). Similarly, it still expends energy embracing the demands of social policy, whether or not it actually serves the interests of social workers or service users to do so. Going back to both theory and experience, however, we know that 'good practice' – that which genuinely helps struggling children, families and neighbourhoods – is on offer in many teams and organisations. Among other things, it is associated with: concern, care and therapeutic support; productive relationships; respect and transparency; willingness to reframe assumptions (eg about the nature of social problems, about professional power and 'empowerment', and 'involuntary' service users); intervention at both individual and community levels; and commitment to collective solutions (Ferguson and Woodward, 2009; Healy and Darlington, 2009; Gallagher, 2010; Fargion, 2012; Rogowski, 2012b; Teater and Baldwin, 2012).

Conclusion

Ten years ago, Mark Lymbery (2011, p 381) suggested that social work was 'at the crossroads', facing either a future of moral bankruptcy or one with a 'sense of mission'. Today, social work is still at that crossroads (Lavalette, 2011b). Social work with children and families remains in a fragile state, lacking courage and conviction and too concerned with contentious policy discourses. While this thing called social work is lagging behind, there is a growing body of evidence to suggest that social workers, when working alongside service users, are not! Although space and opportunity are limited, and many families will, understandably, continue to react to social work intervention with fear and hostility, at least at first (Gallagher, 2010), children and families social workers are finding opportunities for progressive practice (Ferguson and Woodward, 2009; Rogowski, 2012a). So, too, are students and educators (Woodward and Mackay, 2011), while collective resistance to social injustice is building (Lavalette, 2011b) and service users' voices are beginning to be heard (Beresford and Hasler, 2009). As Paul says, there is hope that another social work is possible. In the current climate, however, this possibility of progressive social work needs to translate into reality. Social work did not stand up to the Thatcherite neoliberal programme or to New Labour's version of it, but the UK is now facing a new and brutal neoliberal assault. Social work with children and families continues to operate in contested, emotive places, but, in doing so, it is uniquely placed to resist.

Notes

[1] 'The Children's Hearings System is the care and justice system for Scotland's children and young people. A fundamental principle is that children who commit offences, and children who need care and protection, are dealt with in the same system – as these are often the same children.' Quotation from: http://www.scra.gov.uk/children_s_hearings_system/index.cfm

[2] I use the word 'radical' loosely here on the understanding that radical ideas are only one potentially progressive perspective in social work. Notions of criticality, creativity, challenge and resistance in social work come from a variety of political and practice perspectives.

Rights and wrongs: young citizens in a young country

Mark Drakeford and Ian Butler

Paul Michael Garrett's conclusions about the future prospects of social work strike us as both too pessimistic and too optimistic at the same time. We are more optimistic about the possibilities of creating a more sympathetic policy environment in which a more fruitful social work practice could be developed, but also more pessimistic about the potential of the profession itself to deliver such a form of practice.

Writing from Wales, we will concentrate on tracing the development of child and family policies and practice here in the post-devolution era. In doing so, we draw some points of comparison and contrast with the Garrett analysis of the same field in England and the Republic of Ireland.

Garrett rightly points out that the neo-conservative project, which has exercised a hegemonic grip over large parts of the developed world for more than 30 years, is as much about social policy as it is about economics. Cuts in public expenditure and widening inequalities are often presented as the inevitable by-products of unavoidable and overriding policy purposes – the regrettable but inescapable consequences of dealing with crises such as the level of public indebtedness. We would agree that such outcomes are not by-products at all, but the inherent techniques and purposes of the 'neo-con' project. Cuts are not a temporary response to immediate dangers, but part of a long-term determination to redraw the contract between the citizen and the state. Widening inequalities are not a matter of hand-wringing regret, but an intentional policy tool of an outlook which believes that a market economy should reward success and punish failure.

In Garrett's analysis, such trends appear irresistible. Partly, at least, this is because Garrett takes an over-deterministic view of ideological hegemony. Even in the time in which the authors have been involved in social work, both the context in which social work is practised and the practice of social work itself have shifted (see, among many others, Hendrick, 1994; Butler and Drakeford, 2005a). Hegemonies shift and can be shifted in the future. In that sense, our position is closer to Garrett's early endorsement of the Bourdieussian proposition that the state is a continuous battlefield, rather than (as the text goes on to imply) a place where the battle has already been concluded in favour of neoliberalisation. In Wales, we believe, resistance has been possible and, albeit to a limited extent, successful, which demonstrates that such a deterministic pessimism need not be taken for granted.

Ever since it was first established in 1999, the National Assembly for Wales has been an institution in development. The powers that are exercised by the fourth Assembly, elected in May 2011, are wider, both in scope and depth, than any of its predecessors (see Butler and Drakeford, 2010). Yet, policy directed at children and young people is one of those areas where powers were transferred in their entirety from the outset. Thus, the details that Garrett traces in relation, for example, to 'Quality Protects' and 'Every Child Matters' have never applied in Wales (see Butler and Drakeford, 2010; Butler, 2011). This is not to argue, of course, that Welsh policymaking takes place in a vacuum, or in a way that is immune from influences elsewhere. The legacy of the long Thatcher years, for example, applied as much to public services in Wales as in England. Nevertheless, it is our contention that, against that background, more than a decade of policy development can now be traced that, cumulatively, amounts to a distinctively Welsh approach to social welfare generally, and social work with children and families, in particular.

The task of shaping such a policy approach began early in the life of the Assembly, with a formal decision to adopt the principles set out in the United Nations Convention on the Rights of the Child (UNCRC) (Welsh Assembly Government, 2000, 2002, 2007). The application of these principles in the Welsh context was set out in a

2002 document, *Rights to action* (Welsh Assembly Government, 2002), which identified seven 'core aims' for children and young people, to:

- have a flying start in life;
- have a comprehensive range of education and learning opportunities;
- enjoy the best possible health and be free from abuse, victimisation and exploitation;
- have access to play, leisure, sporting and cultural activities;
- be listened to, treated with respect and have their race and cultural identity recognised;
- have a safe home and a community that supports physical and emotional well-being; and
- not be disadvantaged by poverty.

It is beyond the scope of this brief response to set out all the practical actions taken to translate these rights into action (although the detail is available, see, eg, Butler, 2011). In the direct field of social welfare, the results can be seen in services provided to some of the most troubled young people. Garrett provides disturbing evidence of the extent to which institutional responses in the Republic remain a first rather than a last resort in responding to young people, despite its utterly disreputable history. In Wales (as in other parts of the UK), this trend has been reversed in important ways. While Garrett reports that at least 100 children under the age of 18 were admitted to adult psychiatric facilities in 2010, the equivalent figure in Wales was nine, and was falling. In the same way, as far as young people in trouble with the law are concerned, there have been consistent falls in the numbers of first-time entrants to the youth justice system in Wales, while the number of young people sentenced to custody has fallen from 185 in April 2004 to 143 in February 2009, a period when rates of offending and reoffending were both also in decline (for details, see Drakeford, 2010).

More generally, among the more important developments of the rights agenda in Wales have been the establishment of the first-ever office of Children's Commissioner and of Funky Dragon, the peer-led organisation that directly gives a voice to children and young people in Welsh policymaking and that submitted two independent reports to the 2008 United Nations periodic review of children's rights in the UK. The most significant single example is, arguably, to be found in the Rights of Children and Young Persons (Wales) Measure 2011, in which the National Assembly made early use of newly acquired powers to pass primary legislation. The Measure, when fully implemented by 2014, will place a duty on Welsh ministers and other public bodies in Wales to have 'due regard' for the UNCRC in everything they do.

To summarise: Welsh policymaking in the devolution era has been founded on the assumption that children and young people are rights-holders, with an entitlement to participate in decisions on matters that affect them. This approach is now embedded in primary legislation, reflecting an established policy orientation that operates right across all of those in the 'children's workforce'.

In Wales, the basic context within which social work is practised also needs to be set out briefly. Here, social work remains a local authority responsibility. There are no Children's Trusts in Wales and no hiving off of older people's services to health bodies. Social workers remain within the local authority family because of the additional leverage that this provides in their role as brokers, negotiating alongside families with services such as housing and education. Successive Welsh governments have emphasised a preference for cooperation, rather than competition, as the best means of bringing about service improvement, and social work's enduring place within local authorities is intended to enhance the chances of it developing and sustaining collaborative working relationships with other services that shape the lives of service users (see Morgan, 2002; Drakeford, 2007a, 2007b; Sullivan, 2007; Marquand, 2008; Stead, 2008; Davies and Williams, 2009).

In that task, social work is regarded as a profession best carried out by well-trained, reflexive practitioners, encouraged to exercise informed judgement in conditions of continuous complexity. The character of those judgements is itself shaped by the overriding rejection of market principles as a basis for providing public services in Wales. In a market, as Garrett illustrates, social work itself can soon be privatised, with relationships between user and provider reduced to the low-trust consumerism inherent in the economic rationalities that underpin neoliberalism. In contrast, the ambition for public services in Wales is that they engender high-trust relationships between workers and citizens, based on an understanding that results are best when each is recognised as making an equally important contribution to such encounters (Butler and Drakeford, 2005b). Social workers and their users bring different things to the table (as do doctors and their patients, teachers and their students), but what they bring is equally important to relationships based on mutuality, respect and a joint production of best outcomes. These are ambitions, of course, rather than achieved realities. The daily exigencies of practice remain shaped in Wales, as elsewhere, by the cash-starved nature of public services. Yet, our argument remains that both the general and specific contexts of social welfare practice in Wales in the post-devolution era provide some grounds for optimism that the 'space' for a different sort of social work, for which Garrett calls, can be created.

If the foregoing suggests that a different set of policy possibilities are still capable of being pursued, even in a place where the impact of neoliberalism across the border remains a daily fact of life, our position on social work itself is rather more pessimistic than Garrett appears to suggest. Social work's main vulnerability, he seems to suggest, lies in its 'left-leaning' reputation, which places the profession at odds with the new orthodoxies shared across England and the Irish Republic. In the English context, he illuminates that position in an account of the Cameron Conservative Party's 'attempts to re-enchant' social work, by offering it a place in the socially benign depositions of the Big Society. While rightly warning against a simple view of social work as an inherently benign and emancipatory activity, Garrett nevertheless positions these new overtures to social work as representing a new alignment, in which the profession is vulnerable to seduction away from its instinctive egalitarianism.

In fact, it could just as well be argued that the dominant strand in social work's history has been the conservative individualism so characteristic of its Charity Organisation Society origins. Far from being a new Conservative enthusiasm of the Cameron era, the strongest political support for social work in the post-war era has come from that party. The first major child welfare scandal of the period occurred in 1973 with the death of Maria Colwell (Butler and Drakeford, 2011). The Secretary of State at the time was Sir Keith Joseph, later Mrs Thatcher's ideological guru. His response was to emphasise the importance of social work. The Whitehawk estate, where Maria lived and died, was well-known in Brighton as a place where families struggled against the great shaping forces of unemployment, poverty, poor housing and ill-health. None of that featured in Sir Keith's thinking. He argued, instead, that the greatest policy challenge was to understand the post-war paradox, in which 30 years of the welfare state had failed to eradicate Beveridge's 'five giants' of want, idleness, squalor, ignorance and disease. The answer, Sir Keith believed, included a substantially extended role for social work, in which both help and social discipline could be applied to those families where problems were passed down from generation to generation. Such an analysis, where the cause of social difficulties is located within the lives of those who experience them, has continued to be attractive to Conservative politicians ever since. It has an impact on the sort of social worker who needs to be recruited for such purposes – the no-nonsense 'Mums Army' of Virginia Bottomley in the 1990s, as much as the retired bankers cited by Garrett as the social workers of choice among current Coalition ministers. It was exactly in response to this sort of thinking that Barbara Castle, in her famous diaries (Castle, 1980), declared, 'Thank God I am a socialist and not a social worker'. In doing so, she echoed the views of the founder of the welfare state, William Beveridge. As a young man, before the First World War, he was sent to provide social work in one of the poorest communities in the East End of London. The experience made a profound impression upon him. As he later wrote: 'if anyone ever thought that colossal evils could be remedied by small doses of culture and charity and amiability, I for one do not think so now' (quoted in Silburn, 1991, p 81).

The point we make is simply that relying on a revival of social work's own 'emancipatory' tradition is too slender a reed on which to rely for a sufficient answer to Garrett's final question, and the perennial dilemma of social work, 'What is, therefore, to be done?' (see Butler and Drakeford, 2012). In this brief response, we hope that we have demonstrated that context shapes content in social work, just as it does in the lives of social work users. The conditions of neoliberalism are inimical to a social work based on mutuality, trust, respect and a set of shared citizenship rights, because neoliberalism itself rejects such values. An activity called social work can be practised in such circumstances, but is likely to be animated by a set of disciplinary purposes designed to ensure that those cut off from the benefits enjoyed by others in a sharply unequal society are reconciled to their lot with the minimum of cost or disruption to others. The sort of social work practice that Garrett and we favour can only flourish in circumstances characterised by broader social-democratic principles and policies. Social work in Wales faces many challenges and disappointments, but it is still possible to have some optimism about its future – not because of a reliance on its own inherent radicalism, but because the wider policy context in Wales is one that makes such radicalism possible.

Social Justice social work struggles in Canada: poverty, neoliberalism and symbolic resistance

Donna Baines

In his lead article in this book, Garrett notes historical and contemporary differences between England and Ireland, many of which find their roots in colonialism. Similarly, with the exception of First Nations people, the country currently known as Canada has deep colonial roots and tends to avoid discussions about occupying stolen land. The post-colonial/colonial relationship shapes many of the realities of the lives of First Nations and non-First Nations peoples (Kulchyski et al., 1999; Blackstock, 2010; Freeman, 2011). Based in the local, social work theory and practice have been slow to address the complexities of colonialism and the global political economies that sustain and benefit from it, but it is appropriate that critical social work texts weave these themes in from the start. In Canada, First Nations people are disproportionately involved with the child welfare system, reflecting their impoverishment, misrepresentation and marginalisation within the larger economic, political and social systems (Blackstock and Trocme, 2005).

Other kinds of post- and neocolonial relations are also evident in the kinds of exploitive relationships most of the global North has with (un)developing countries and our governments' unwillingness to assist Third World countries in humanitarian efforts or to support fair and sustainable development (Reader, 1999; Gardiner, 2007). The same inequity is echoed in the ways that many immigrants and refugees to Canada find themselves at the bottom of the labour market, pushed to the edges of our racially stratified society (Galabuzzi, 2006).

—

Garrett poses two strong challenges to social work in his lead article. First, he asserts that it is 'misguided to simply view social work – with children and families or any other group – as an entirely benign and emancipatory activity'. He goes on to note that although most social workers are employed by the state, the state cannot be assumed to be a neutral body. Rather, in most instances, its role is 'to maintain the present ordering of economic relations'. While I agree that the state orders economic relations, it also attempts to reorder social and political relations, and its policies and practices reflect the relative strength of social forces and the successes and failures of the struggles they have pursued to meet their various interests (Panitch, 1994; Beiler and Morton, 2003). More than not benign, the state is not static: it is a site of contestation and struggle, and fortunately one that we can influence, although this influence has ebbed as democratic processes have been systematically shut down in the era of neoliberalism (Harvey, 2005; Fraser, 2010). Further, as the state privatises and social services are shifted to the voluntary and private sectors, the number of social workers employed directly by the state is decreasing rapidly. However, as the state adopts pro-market priorities for its delivery and management of social services and extends its control through funding contracts in the voluntary and for-profit sectors, it is increasingly difficult to discern differences between the three (Baines, 2004b; McDonald, 2006; Carey, 2009).

Garrett also suggests that social work is always being remade and there is no such thing as a timeless recourse to an authentic form of practice'. Indeed, it is important to recognise that much of social work is not and never was about social justice or fairness. As a so-called professional practice, social work has always been a pluralistic discipline with starkly different streams of practice often operating in opposition to each other (Baines, 2011). Some of these streams reflect charitable roots and the 'scientific' delivery of the early Charitable Organisation Societies (Carniol, 2010), while others promote mainstream practices and analysis, and still others critique both these streams, offering instead models rooted in equity, full participation and justice for all (Lundy, 2011). Currently, in Canada, accreditation standards for post-secondary social work programmes require engagement with anti-oppressive practice (AOP) and theory (Canadian Association of Schools of Social Work, 2012), making this the 'official' though not necessarily dominant practice model. AOP recognises the simultaneous contestation and mutual reinforcement of multiple oppressive relations operating within any given scenario. These multiple oppressions include class, race, gender, sexual orientation, disability, age and so forth. As this model has been institutionalised through accreditation standards and broader, 'professional' discussions, many fear that it has lost much of its dynamism and capacity to be a politicised response to both emerging and long-standing issues. Many social justice-oriented social work schools and practitioners use similar terms and concepts, such as critical, structural or radical social work, to describe multi-strand, multi-approach, politicised engagements with social work theory and practice (Carniol, 2010; Lundy, 2011).

The label we attach to critical approaches is less important than the fact that we engage in a battle of ideas and make spaces for innovative practices and policies based in fairness and social justice. Indeed, much of the struggle at this point in time is symbolic (Bourdieu, 1991), as we work to overcome the individualism, elitism and exclusion that has been aggressively woven into our societies since the advent of neoliberalism in the 1980s (Harvey, 2005). Neoliberal economic policies led to the general financial crisis of 2008 and the painful recessions in the ensuing years, accelerating the polarisation of wealth and poverty and precipitous declines in funding for services to reduce inequities between social groups and classes (Nikoloski, 2011; Giroux, 2012). As Garrett notes, citing Bourdieu (2001), 'we are enduring "a conservative revolution"'.

Garrett also argues that we are facing a crisis in safeguarding children. A large part of this crisis emanates from a lack of good employment options and the concomitant lack of support services for families and children. In Canada, one in 10 people continue to live in poverty, or 639,000 children and their families (Campaign 2000, 2012). Poverty is particularly high in Canada's larger cities. For example, in Toronto, the largest city, one in four families was defined as low-income in 2005, up from one in six in 1990 (United Way of Toronto, 2007). Similarly, non-standard or precarious employment is also growing and is particularly acute in larger cities, with Toronto reporting that between 1997 and 2006, temporary employment increased from 9.7% of the labour force to 13.4% (United Way of Toronto, 2007).

Many families and children find themselves in very challenging circumstances, unable to find decent, or in many cases any, employment and faced with few supports and a tide of human service cutbacks. The space permitted this response precludes a detailed discussion of the history of child welfare in Canada, although it is commonly thought of as having moved through three stages: (1) early voluntary (1870s to 1945); (2) early child welfare and government intervention (1946 to 1964); and (3) legislative recognition of society's responsibility to protect children and detailed legislation on how to deliver this support (1985 to present) (Lero and Kyle, 1991). Under Canada's federalist system, child welfare is a provincial responsibility and legislation varies greatly across the 10 provinces and two territories. However, in most regions, legislation changed in the late 1990s from 'least restrictive' measures to 'least disruptive' and 'child-focused'. Admissions doubled in many places and despite funding formulas recognising increased volume, 50 of the 52 Children's Aid Societies ran a deficit in Ontario, Canada's most populated province, making it difficult for social workers to provide care and support to families and leaving families in often desperate situations (Baines, 2004b). By the end of the following decade, legislation changed again, with greater emphasis placed on keeping families together, 'better outcomes for children' and 'differential responses' to cases depending on needs and severity. Despite improved wording in the latest child welfare policy Acts, it is economic and labour market policy changes that would make the biggest difference in the lives of most families and children, as it is poverty, an eroded public education system, minimalist services with long waiting lists and inadequate resources, and a lack of good employment opportunities that shape the harsh realities that impact on the lives of those involved in the child welfare systems in Canada.

The language of outcomes (noted earlier) reflects the neoliberal turn in social service provision, particularly the standardising practices of performance and New Public Management (Baines, 2004a). Although these managerialised models purport to emphasise 'best practices', in reality, by focusing on cost-effective, risk-minimising, time-precise practices, they eliminate forms of practice associated with the difficult-to-quantify outcomes of social justice-oriented social work practice, such as advocacy, policy analysis, social critique, community mobilisation, service user empowerment and collegial solidarity (Carey, 2009; Baines, 2011; Lundy, 2011). Citing Bellamy Foster (1998, p ix), Garrett notes the '"prevailing social order's systematic tendency to create unsatisfying work"'. Although always contested and difficult, under performance management and its computerised risk assessments and tightly timed timelines and report submission, child welfare work has been standardised to the point that many workers feel that they have lost their voice and professional discretion, resulting in high levels of stress and alienation from their work (Baines, 2004b; Smith, 2007).

Child welfare workers are not alone in this experience. Research from a four-country study of restructuring in the voluntary social services shows commonalities between and among the study sites, including: increased pace and volume of work; increased use of a flexible and impermanent labour force, such as contract, part-time, casual, split-shift and on-call; increased workplace violence against workers; a growing sense among workers that they have few opportunities to use social justice skills or analysis on the job; and an overall increase in workplace stress, illness, burn-out and staff turnover (Baines et al, 2011; Baines and Cunningham, 2011). The situation of child welfare and other social workers is unlikely to improve in the short term, as employers pursue 'free market' strategies and attack the wages, pensions and benefits of those who provide public or quasi-public services. Despite claims that many organisations are pursuing evidence-based practice, there is little or no evidence to show that outcomes-driven work is more effective and a great deal of evidence suggests that the field of social work is narrowing, polarised between good and bad jobs, and increasingly stressful (Baines et al, 2011; Bates,

2011). A substantial body of literature shows that many social workers continue to resist the standardisation of work and try to insert care and social analysis into their work, although most of these actions remain individual, dispersed (Carey, 2009; Baines, 2010; Ross, 2011) and, as Smith (2007, p 152) notes, 'come in under the radar'.

How can those seeking a social justice agenda within children's services, practice with First Nations people and other areas of social work tap into the resistance and resilience of those working to build a collective agenda of social change and fairness? Findings from the four-country study mentioned earlier highlight similarities as well as ongoing differences between and among welfare states and social work delivery systems, suggesting that globalisation is not monolithic and that some jurisdictions have experienced significant success in defending services and pre- or post-neoliberal philosophies and/or resisting New Public Management's prescriptive, Taylorised service models (Baines and Cunningham, 2011; Baines et al, 2011). Similarly, studies of workplace resistance show that personal values and ethics are the primary motivators for those undertaking advocacy, resistance and union activism (Carniol, 2010; Baines, 2011), underscoring the point made earlier in this contribution that much of our struggle today is symbolic (within systems of meaning) and within the realm of ideas.

Bonnie Freeman (2011) argues that anti-oppressive social work practice and First Nations practice have much to teach each other, although, to date, there is little written from this perspective. In the case of child and family services, First Nations groups have argued that self-determination must be the principle underlying models of child welfare service and care, and that child welfare practices need to reflect the resilience of First Nations communities, traditional practices and engagement with contemporary struggles (Blackstock and Trocme, 2005; Blackstock, 2010). These themes are important in the context of the increasing global mobility of people and the growing diversity of Canada and other countries. Social justice-oriented social work practice can certainly benefit from: (1) a stronger recognition of the role history plays in shaping the everyday lives of numerous groups in society, but particularly First Nations people; (2) the strength of non-capitalist ways of living and understanding the world; and (3) the resilience of those fighting post-colonialism and late-day capitalism for a more equitable and hopeful future.

In order to be connected to the changing conditions and social justice struggles in society, social work practice and theory need to be constantly growing, changing and tested against the realities in which service users and their communities exist. Many forms of resistance once thought integral to radical practice (Bailey and Brake, 1975; Brake and Bailey, 1980) are seen as no longer possible or very difficult within the neoliberalised workplace (Ferguson, 2004; Smith, 2007; Ross, 2011). Fortunately, new possibilities, such as social or community unionism (Baines, 2010) or the Occupy Movement, provide useful incubators for radical debate and new practices to arise, tailor-made to fit today's conditions and 'glocal' challenges (Giroux, 2012). I recently asked my social justice and social work class to visit an Occupy site or another major social protest and to observe what was happening and who was debating what. It was interesting to see how very easy it was for students to find an Occupy activity or other major protest event to attend and how much they learned. A number of studies suggest that social protest is on the increase, although it is often sporadic (ie happening independently of major long-term strategies or movements), episodic (responding to a specific incident or new issue) and organised in ways that veteran activists do not always recognise (Raasch-Gilman, 2012). Although social workers and social work academics put in long hours on their paid work, we need to be directly involved in these new debates and forms of struggle. They test our theory and provide an incentive to remain current and on the fighting edge of issues rather than trailing behind, analysing issues and struggles already irrelevant. They keep us from getting routinised in our resistance and provide a useful antidote to the wearying experience of the last two decades, where, despite our resistance to neoliberalism, little or nothing much seemed to ever change for the better. Finally, they can feed our sense of optimism and help to build the new social justice practices and insights required by today's rapidly changing socio-political environment.

—

'What is to be done?'

Roger Smith

The infernal logic of 'the market' has undoubtedly created a spirit of despondency, and this clearly infuses Paul Michael Garrett's deliberations on the state and prospects for social work in England and the Irish Republic. Direct and sustained attacks on the well-being of the very elements of the population with whom social work is most concerned are bound to have material consequences, and social work itself will be at the forefront of the task of resolving the problems that this will generate. At the same time, of course, welfare spending is also threatened, and both statutory and non-statutory forms of intervention are being undermined. To use the language of the market, as demand increases inexorably, so supply is being choked off.

The bleak picture painted for us is undoubtedly realistic, and this acts as an important reminder that social work operates in a world widely characterised by inequality and oppression. However, it becomes dangerous if it gives rise to no more than 'radical pessimism' (Butler and Pugh, 2004) and a pervasive sense that nothing can be done. Garrett's article tries to rise above this in its final sentences, with a call for a new range of 'possibilities founded on total opposition' to the rampant forces of neoliberalism to which we are currently exposed. For social work, as he acknowledges, this task involves challenging structural power bases and the hegemonic capacity of those who set the agenda for practice. The Social Work Action Network in Britain has begun to articulate a contemporary voice of challenge, and offers at least the hope of a new dynamic of change.

By its very existence, social work represents an acknowledgement that 'something is wrong' within our society. Its origins in Victorian philanthropy speak ambiguously of the modern welfare project being grounded in mixed motives, including middle-class guilt or fear, the demands of social reproduction and the capitalist economy, the desire for social control, and, of course, the demands and actions of people and communities experiencing disadvantage and oppression. These and subsequent strands of thought and ideology have been ever present, if in modified form, in the development and modification of the social work function in the modern era. As such, of course, it is possible to identify continuing strands of resistance and opposition, and a readiness within social work to act on the evidence encountered directly by practitioners to provide evidence and articulate the need for change. Nowhere is the ambiguity embedded in social work's very existence more clearly demonstrated than in its response to service users' frustration and anger at not being listened to. Social workers have been criticised for their shortcomings in this respect; yet, it is social work as much as any other professional grouping that has responded to criticism and attempted to embed a requirement to take account of service users' wishes and feelings in its principles and practice. This tension is exemplified by the work of Peter Beresford, for example, who has both challenged the readiness of practitioners to exclude service users in some cases, quite rightly, but also acknowledged that social work is capable of 'listening' and being a friend and advocate.

That social work has the capacity to promote genuine change should not be doubted, and it may help here to pause to reflect on its achievements, as well as its potential, in order to support the belief that it has a demonstrable role in advocating for and achieving change, and that this role has been and can be effective. 'Radical social work', of course, dates back at least to the 1970s, and its influence can be traced throughout the intervening years. This continuity of achievement can be characterised in several distinct ways: awareness, solidarity, resistance and transformation. That is to say, social work has a track record of 'making a difference' not only for individuals in difficult circumstances, but also for identifiable groups and segments of the population who experience oppression and disadvantage, and it has made a difference in a number of ways, which remain practicable, even in highly adverse circumstances:

1. *Awareness:* By its very nature, social work comes into contact with examples of injustice and harm on a routine basis. It is arguable, therefore, that this provides a continuing opportunity to draw the attention of wider interests to this evidence. It could indeed be argued, for instance, that social work has played a significant part, through practice and research, in generating wider awareness of the extent and impact of domestic violence. While it must be acknowledged that social work has also been subject to criticism for its limited response, this does not entirely discredit the positive contribution it has made in drawing attention to this issue and articulating principles of good practice.

2. *Solidarity:* Despite the individualising tendencies of the structural frameworks within which contemporary Western social work is practised, there also remain opportunities to engage with groups and communities in ways that recognise their inherent strengths and support efforts to promote cooperation and empowerment. Insofar as groupwork, for example, has been developed and rethought, it now clearly demonstrates the capacity to validate and build on the experiences of excluded populations, notably, in models of practice with young people sharing common characteristics, such as having been in care.

3. *Resistance:* Social work has an established tradition of 'resistance' in the sense of non-compliance with oppressive and potentially harmful impositions on service users. Where stereotypes and stigma compromise the treatment of people who use services, social workers are often well placed to utilise their value base to challenge potentially damaging preconceptions about people who use services. Social work is also well placed to draw on the language and instruments of human rights, and to utilise these to support individual and collective actions to challenge breaches of these international commitments.

4. *Transformation:* Opportunities for major transformations in practice, or in the circumstances of people who use services, are clearly limited, especially in the current climate, as Paul Michael Garrett demonstrates. However, social work does have a role to play, notably,

—

in localised and relatively small-scale initiatives to empower groups and communities, reshape services, and develop new ways of understanding and addressing the problems impacting on people's lives.

As Garrett makes clear, however, the opportunities for progressive actions of this kind are severely curtailed in a context of retrenchment and a determined 'squeeze' on incomes and other resources. In fact, the demand for social work intervention is likely to be intensified under present circumstances, even as the resources available to support it are diminished. Social workers, however, have a value base to rely on that remains the bedrock for practice that is committed to those who are vulnerable, victimised or oppressed. It remains highly effective in acting in the interests of people of all ages in these circumstances, despite populist myth-making to the contrary. However, insofar as this positive involvement is restricted to individual 'cases' and constructed in this form in thought and deed, the capacity for social work to act as a driver for positive change is limited. Social work must be prepared to make connections, between, say, the circumstances of the many children who are 'neglected', drug users in abandoned communities or those older people who become 'isolated'. In the first instance, social work is, as suggested earlier, ideally placed to document and make the necessary linkages between these examples of 'unmet need', and to make the case for more than just emergency action to address the 'symptoms' of systematic impoverishment.

Social work and the sociological imagination

Stanley Houston

One of the significant gaps in modern social work is the lack of an embedded 'sociological imagination': one that irrefutably draws the connection between private ills and public issues; one that debunks political rhetoric and deconstructs ideology. The connection between private ills (the suffering of a growing underclass) and public issues (as defined by the state) comes into sharper focus through the traditional Marxist idea that 'base' irredeemably impacts on 'superstructure'. Applying this to the modern world reveals that neoliberalism has a profound effect on human lives and the manner and shape in which welfare regimes are constructed. Whenever neoliberal doctrines have been applied, inequalities grow *tout court*, the environment suffers and there is a much greater propensity for war as nation-states struggle to find new markets.

Neoliberalism is often portrayed as a quasi-science by its adherents. For example, it is argued that the market (working to a set of immutable laws) will perform best if left alone by government, that the rising tide of wealth will lift both yachts and sailing dinghies through the 'trickle-down effects' of Friedman-esque macroeconomics. Such assumptions have failed abysmally in the face of tsunami-type economic decline. The myth of the free market was so palpably exposed when George Bush Jr was forced to bail out American banks to the sum of several hundred billion dollars following the most recent crash in the global economy. Yet, incredibly, this was justified by the argument that free marketeers must *occasionally* prop up the economy during periods of recession – that this had been part of neoliberal doctrines all along.

Combined with this impoverished grasp of the sociological imagination in social work is the lack of an iconoclastic voice, a modern-day Jeremiah (in the social work wilderness), willing to challenge the sacred cows and taken-for-granted shibboleths of contemporary, quotidian social work: someone who might write with 'attitude' and administer the sting of a Socratic Gadfly; someone unafraid of critique; someone rejecting piecemeal, reformist alternatives as yet another sop or palliative or ideological ruse; someone ready to make the diagnosis that macroeconomics must be understood if we are to appraise the continuing and perhaps growing malaise affecting social work. Iconoclasm must have theoretical substance, though, or it will be so easily dismissed as vacuous ranting.

For me, Paul Michael Garrett's growing and impressive *oeuvre* fills the gaps just mentioned and his latest contribution, to which I am responding, is no exception. What Garrett does so well is to make the crucial link between private ills and public issues with iconoclastic verve, crossing the boundary between critical social policy and critical social theory to add theoretical flesh to his reasoned arguments. This is captured so well is his perspicacious and epiphanic comment (towards the end of the article) that:

> What is required is not a reshaped child protection *system*, but a
> child protection *economy* that serves and safeguards all children....
> Given this project, there is a need to create a different set of
> social and political possibilities founded on total opposition to
> a destabilised and vengeful capitalism.

Garrett's analysis of child and family social work both in the UK and in the Republic of Ireland makes for dismal reading (I found the critical coverage of the Ryan Report to be harrowing). Yet, it reminds the reader that significant progress will not be made unless one understands the deeply rooted mechanisms according to which neoliberal welfare operates: its commodifying tendencies and McDonaldisation effects; its propulsion towards a rampant individualism; its hegemonic appeal to the 'Big Society'. Notably, Britain is currently being governed by a significant number of millionaires from public school backgrounds; yet, rhetorically, what do they really understand about life in underprivileged housing estates? In what way are they qualified to decide on the shape of social work today?

Moreover, Tony Blair's antecedent 'Third Way' variety of neoliberalism, borrowing heavily from Bill Clinton's market globalism, introduced changes to child and family social work and social policy designed to eradicate child poverty through a rejection of state paternalism and an endorsement of 'social partnership'. However, Garrett reminds us that Blairite social policy took on an increasingly authoritarian, panoptical attitude to young people and families defined as anti-social, did not reach its targets in relation to child poverty, and adopted the ruse of modernisation to divert attention away from structural reforms. The massive problems facing the Republic of Ireland, which is attempting to modernise and standardise its welfare services under conditions of extreme economic austerity, present an ominous reality for those marginalised following the collapse of the 'Celtic Tiger'.

So, one might conclude from reading the article that child and family social work in the UK and the Republic of Ireland is in a sorry state. Garrett's arguments and presentation of supportive evidence might unassailably lead to such a conclusion. I do not dispute Garrett's findings, but I do want to register some important points about making use of the sociological imagination in social work and the application of much-needed critique. First of all, reading Garrett's well-crafted article reminded me of the early Frankfurt's School's analysis and critique of capitalism – and how it led to an insidious pessimism. In fact, Adorno felt that the only way of achieving some kind of liberation was through art; not the populist variety found in plastic, one-dimensional American culture, but high art – art from the Renaissance. Clearly, Garrett is not arguing that we resort to Wagner's Ring for inspiration, but there is a heavy sense of pessimism emanating from his critical summary. Towards the end of the article, he makes a limited attempt to address change, referring to the need to form alliances and engaging in 'oppositional social work'.

—

My view is that the sociological imagination in social work needs to move beyond pessimism to offer concrete, thought-through strategies for change and resistance that can be understood by social work practitioners and that resonate with them. Unless we do this, there is a danger of compounding the poor morale in social work that many argue is at an all-time low. Pessimism is insidious, contagious and self-perpetuating. It can lead to a mindset of 'learned helplessness', particularly when the profession is atomised. But more than this, the profession needs to adopt an enabling mindset – a way of making sense of the constraints facing them. This places a heavy responsibility on the social work academe to present emancipatory frameworks and ideas that reframe possibilities for change and build social work leadership. Had Garrett taken this further step – a step towards envisioning change, conceptually, enticingly, with the prospect of meaningful praxis to follow – then the iconoclasm he embodies in this piece would have reached its apogee.

To this end, I suggest that social work might be understood in the context of three governing, juxtaposed parameters: the state, civil society and professional ideology. Within these parameters, social work has a degree of *occupational space* – arguably, a truncated space, yet one that is ever present. The possibilities of this space are determined to a large extent by the shifting flux within each of the parameters. Thus, there are continuing changes within the state, even though it is neoliberal to its core in its current manifestation. Yet, Blairite social policy presented differing hues compared with contemporary, Cameron-inspired directives. Civil society, in Greece and elsewhere, is showing strong oppositional voices to global capitalism. Professional ideology is ever-changing, embracing a diversifying range of critical perspectives: political social work, anti-oppressive practice, rights-based social work, anti-sectarian social work, anti-racist social work, user and carer empowerment, and structural social work. It is the challenge for the sociological imagination in social work to draw together these different critical strands, teasing out common premises behind them and showing how creative synergies might occur between them.

Within this occupational space, social workers have *discursive* space. In other words, they can *reflect* on the interplay between the 'micro' and 'macro' domains, the interplay between agency and structure, the interface between power and human biography, and how emotion is shaped in human experience. Moreover, they can at least examine the tenuous boundary between the state and civil society and how this presents choices or ways of fulfilling state-mandated requirements yet in a way that maintains and respects the tenets of relationship-based practice. Thus, social workers are uniquely placed to be *boundary spanners*, holding in tension the requirements of the organisational system but being responsive to the needs of the lifeworld and community at the same time. For example, I can complete my Looked After Children review in the mode of state functionary or I can personalise the experience, taking account of the use of language, power differentials and the intersection of different presentations of habitus, field and capital. There is always a choice, to some degree; there is always the capacity to reframe, to some degree. By failing to grasp this essential aspect of our natures, we become inauthentic, part of the Heideggerian herd. Nefarious practice occurs when social workers do not respect the sacrosanctity of the boundary between state and civil society.

Within this occupational and discursive space, one realises the essentially *contradictory* nature of modern, neoliberal welfare. Yes, it continues to roll out a risk-averse, technocratic juggernaut, where regulation and performance management are increasingly to the fore; yet, growing among the weeds are some green shoots of hope, some seminal models of practice. The resolution model (Turnell, 1999) in child protection moves beyond a deficit-led approach, one offsetting stigma and welfare authoritarianism, and working towards creative solutions that revel in consensual decision-making. The Family Group conference model, to provide another example, puts some restraining barriers on the voice of the 'system', creating space for the lifeworld of families, significant others and social networks to discuss what is in the best interests of a child. Essentially, it is the community who can ultimately protect children, not the state. The Family Group

—

Conference model is an emblematic, albeit microcosmic, example of this truism. Moreover, the model is now being transported and adapted to a range of areas, including youth justice. In another vein, rights-based social work must be the chagrin of the new Right and new conservatives who deplore the impact of European legislative directives on the state and civil society.

Capitalism requires legitimation and one of the ways it gains this is through welfare appeasement. Therein lies the contradiction, because appeasement has to embrace some aspects of a humanising discourse for it to succeed. It would be hard to argue that all aspects of the 'Every Child Matters' policy, which Garrett refers to, are duplicity tainted by hegemonic ideology. Discourses are by no means uniform. Neoliberal discourse, powerful as it is, meets countervailing discourses driven by egalitarianism and justice as part of a human rights culture. Social workers must work with these contradictions, embracing the notion of the *dialectic of control*. This refers to the two-way nature of power, whereby the most disadvantaged are normally able to effect some control over the most advantaged. Purely alienative forms of power are rare, so is unadulterated compliance. Contradiction and resolution are quintessential laws underlying all forms of general development, to return to Marx.

Social workers can gainfully adopt critical, systemic perspectives when attempting to operationalise this dialectical logic. Important here is renewed contact with communities and resistant diversifying elements in civil society. On a grander stage is the need to strengthen international alliances and build solidarity. In this regard, Garrett does recognise the importance of a European nexus. Additionally, within the agency, as a systemic domain, social workers can plan for change. This is to confront the widespread atomisation that afflicts the profession in their daily organisational lives.

In all of this, it is perhaps naive to view social workers as progressive defenders of change, working unproblematically with gusto as catalysts for human emancipation due to the daily nature of their work with the oppressed. Nor should we subscribe to the notion that social workers simply reproduce the prevailing order, acting as the soft cops of the neoliberal bulwark. But we might creatively see them as adopting a contradictory position (Rojek et al, 1988): one that contemporaneously acts as an agent of state control, yet, at the same time, attempts to usurp its harmful effects through an overriding commitment to the sociological imagination. This imagination presents us with the 'right view' but it must be linked (to state boldly the *sine qua non*) with a grounded conceptualisation of 'right action'.

Lost in Arcadia?

Griet Roets and Rudi Roose

In his highly interesting and provocative article, Paul Michael Garrett gives a detailed sketch of recently emerging developments in social work with children and families in England and the Republic of Ireland. Underpinned by Gramscian ideas, Garrett asserts that it is vital to focus on the molecular details associated with the current project of creating a new *hegemony* in the sector that is influenced by the discourse of reform, operating within different professional, expert and emotional registers in the field. Our rejoinder should be considered as an attempt to share some situated reflections and issues that are emerging from our research praxis in Flanders (the Dutch-speaking part of Belgium). Only recently, we have positioned our work (inspired by the French philosopher Camus and the Belgian philosophers Apostel and Hertmans) as a productive and meaningful engagement with complexity and ambiguity as vital elements of social work, since:

> every answer to social problems remains incomplete in any case because it is, in a sense, just an answer that opens up new possibilities, questions and limitations. Nevertheless, the question might be more essential than the answer, as every answer holds the potential to shift evident meanings and to transform realities into provocative issues. (Roose et al, 2011, p 9)

In our point of view, Garrett situates social work justly as rooted in contemporary issues of major socio-economic, political and ideological changes, referring to the global economic crisis that has led to emergency measures providing for greater welfare state intervention, which seems to run entirely counter to the rhetoric of neoliberalism. We follow Garrett's argument when he aptly observes that:

> However, the 'price to be paid' for such initiatives will be met, according to the dominant neoliberal rationality, by the working class and the unemployed poor, who form the core group involved with social work services, particularly those engaging with children and families....
>
> the unfolding and unresolved economic crisis is now being utilised to *reinforce* economic cleavages and deepen class inequalities.

Since the Belgian record of 545 days until the formation of a new federal government, which was formally achieved on 10 December 2011, the unprecedented public expenditure cuts in social security and social services speak volumes. In the context of the current Belgian state reform, the significant example of reforming the child benefit system implies the economic rationality that dominates the debate in our parliament. Supported by civil society actors, proponents suggest that the state should take advantage of the transfer of authority over the child benefit system by implementing three stringent regulations: cutting down child benefit allowances; privatising the procedure to attribute child benefit allowances; and incorporating incentives for targeted populations, such as families in poverty and welfare dependants, to steer them into 'appropriate behaviour'. The schizophrenic cynicism is that the proponents of supporting conditionality in benefit entitlements, which clearly implies an erosion of social protection and encourages new forms of social exclusion while exacerbating the gap between the 'winners' and the 'losers' in our country (Cantillon, 2011), do so under cover of a sly rhetoric of eradicating child poverty in the name of children's rights (Reynaert, 2012). The fact that our society embodies the moral ideal of worker-citizens bearing individual responsibility for their own welfare – which is embedded in the notion of the social investment state, where social policy 'focuses on investment rather than on direct provision of economic maintenance, and on equal opportunities rather than on equality of outcomes' (Cantillon, 2011, p 439) – remains out of the picture.

These developments are of specific importance for social work with children and families, as recent research in Belgium confirms the vulnerability of families in poverty to more intrusive social work interventions in child welfare and protection (Bouverne-De Bie et al, 2011). In the context of the above-mentioned developments, buzzwords like 'social innovation', 'reform', 'better management', 'networking' and 'social entrepreneurship' are currently rife in stressing the crucial role of social work in developing effective and efficient strategies for 'resolving' a wide range of social and economic problems. A heavy emphasis is placed on brief and cost-effective social work interventions in the field of child welfare and protection, inspired by so-called innovative principles of empowering, strengths-oriented and solution-focused approaches in partnership with children and families (Roose et al, forthcoming[b]). Nevertheless, our research reveals an ambiguous picture of the ways in which these approaches are put into practice, since social workers often risk reinforcing a process of individualisation (Roose et al, forthcoming[a]). It has been observed that social work in the field of child welfare and protection tends to depoliticise the poverty problem, translating poverty issues at play in families who are struggling to cope with a lack of resources into problems of 'problematic parenting' and a lack of empowerment.

The vital question is, nonetheless, how social work can position itself in this morbid atmosphere. In that vein, Garrett lingers over this tricky question at the end of his essay, wondering what is, in this context, to be done. Therefore, he is hinting at the possibilities for a new radical social work:

> Given this project, there is a need to create a different set of social and political possibilities founded on total opposition to a destabilised and vengeful capitalism. Here, the challenge is to create a European movement intent on building new alliances and to participate in actions that are intent on resisting capital's endeavour to remake and reorder the world. Specifically, in terms

of social work, engaging in such oppositional activity is, of course, a far from easy task because those in positions of structural power (and invested with the power of naming and defining) seek to maintain hegemony and identify what is permissible and what should be 'closed down'.

Although we deem this element of radicalism very necessary and important, we have recently addressed our concern with the ways in which social work can get absorbed by developing and inserting oppositional politics of resistance (see Roose et al, 2011). A single focus on macro-politics of resistance might reduce the complexity of social realities and ambiguous situations in capitalist and neoliberal market economies that produce and reinforce social inequalities. Here, the work of Camus inspires us, as described in *The myth of Sisyphus* (1991 [1955]) in which the hero, Sisyphus, is condemned to repeat forever the same meaningless task of pushing a boulder up a mountain, yet at the top it always rolls down again. This metaphor might be very suitable for social work because Sisyphus's thoughts when marching down the mountain to start anew are particularly interesting: does he want to abandon his ambiguous mission?

Following Camus, this would suggest that the social worker can 'commit suicide', or s/he can turn to religion, or s/he can struggle on. These options refer to the question of whether social work is or is not meaningless, since the existential condition of social work inherently implies a constant struggle to derive meaning from a sense of meaninglessness, as social problems cannot be 'solved' in linear ways by social workers. Committing suicide in social work refers to a rather cynical disbelief in social work, resulting in burnout, blaming clients, drifting into rather more therapeutic positions and so on. However, this disbelief might result from an optimistic belief that there is a better world to win for social work while embodying heroic claims 'about what social work can achieve ... aligned with the radical tradition in social work' (Marston and McDonald, 2012, p 3). This second response might embody an idealist belief in *Arcadia* that results in politics being caught in a nostalgic dream: the activist belief that a utopian dream of a better social work will be experienced as a land full of flowers, fruits and trees, clear water, and singing birds in an atmosphere where an eternal summer prevails, 'only if we can shut the door for the bad guys' (Hertmans, 2011, p 2). Postulating this discourse might lead to frustration when this ideal of social change is not effectively attained and social work remains lost in Arcadia. As Hertmans (2011, p 2) contemplates, the belief in 'an Arcadian rose garden corrupts both citizens and politics, since this idyllic dream lays the foundation of intolerance towards existing social problems'. Therefore, we argue that social work is not solely a victim of these developments and contexts, but should engage in the struggle with the complexity and ambiguity of its work as a political actor that questions, carries and creates the structures in which social work strategically unfolds. For instance, social work in the field of child welfare and protection in Flanders can be seen as a form of private politics, as this social formation has produced official policies and legislation throughout historical developments.

Rather than shouldering the rifle by embodying activist and oppositional polemics and fighting on the barricades, we attempt to also pay attention to the disciplinary and political identity of social work that always remains ambiguous because social work practice is interrelated with changing welfare regimes and prevailing social policy and civil society, and influenced by theory (Lorenz, 2008). Also, Garrett, citing Parton [2000, p 457]), considers social work's 'essentially contested and ambiguous nature' while shaping the relationship between the individual and society being inevitably restricted by the same issues and contexts as the social problems against the backdrop of political and economic contexts in which social work intervenes. As the Belgian philosopher Apostel (1985) asserted, social work might actually be a poor answer to social issues, but we should deal with social issues since we do not have any better answers (yet). In our point of view, we cannot allow ourselves to be blind to the problems of social work in the context of the global social, political and economic crisis, but it might be productive to imagine social work as a happy Sisyphus who struggles with complexity and ambiguity as vital elements of social work practice (Roose et al, 2011). Apostel (1985) observed

—

73

that embracing the ambiguity of social work remains an opportunity because this enables engagement and solidarity in society, and he concludes that we should have this cake and eat it.

Problematising social work: some reactions

Fabian Kessl

Michel Foucault had only little to say explicitly on social work – like he did in *Discipline and punish*, where he introduced education, public assistance and social work alongside medicine and psychology as pillars of normalisation mechanisms (Foucault, 1979, p 306). But Foucault's perspectives can be used to outline a methodological point of view, which Paul Michael Garrett calls for.

From a Foucauldian perspective, we can categorise Paul Michael Garrett's considerations as a radical and critical approach, as a way of problematising present social work. Problematisation is what Foucault called 'the questioning by the philosopher of the present to which he belongs and in relation to which he has to situate himself' (Foucault, 1988, p 88). This is what Paul Michael Garrett's considerations are all about: he is trying to answer the question of the present shape of social work by exemplifying it by social work with children and families in England and the Republic of Ireland.

So, what is social work currently like, according to Garrett? As he has already shown in his detailed study of 2009 (see Garrett, 2009), children's services are in a fundamental process of transformation, a process identified by Garrett through the analytical gaze of the French thinker Pierre Bourdieu as a 'conservative revolution'. In a dialogue with the German writer Günther Grass in 1999, Bourdieu explained this diagnosis of the present in the following way (see Grass and Bourdieu, 2002 [1999]):

> There is a connexion between this sense of having lost the traditions of the Enlightenment and the global triumph of the neoliberal vision. I see neoliberalism as a conservative revolution,

---

as the term was used between the wars in Germany – a strange revolution that restores the past but presents itself as progressive, transforming regression itself into a form of progress. It does this so well that those who oppose it are made to appear regressive themselves. This is something we have both endured: we are readily treated as old-fashioned, 'has-beens', 'throwbacks'.

Following Bourdieu, Garrett's considerations are motivated by re-establishing – you could almost say, refreshing – the tradition of the Enlightenment as a main task for social research in the field of social work and social policy in general. His article can therefore be understood as a warning to all in social work to be aware and recognise the far-reaching dimension of the current 'neoliberal approaches' in social work: 'In this context, therefore, it remains important to understand that those seeking to promote neoliberal approaches are intent on a "long war" and on ensuring that change takes place and becomes embedded over many years, even decades'.

Due to the ongoing transformations in social work, there is a two-part undercurrent in Garrett's considerations: first, and primarily, he is pointing out the main characteristics of what he calls 'the neoliberal project' by analysing it as a process of establishing a 'new hegemony'; and, second, Garrett tries to regain transformation as a critical and radical concept for social work debates and practice.

The transformation to a different or new hegemony, illustrated by Garrett with the changes being promoted within Children's Services in England and the Republic of Ireland, is not simply about a different way of thinking and modelling the existing states in these two countries. Using the Gramscian concept of cultural hegemony, the state is seen by Garrett not only as an arrangement of the governmental coercive apparatus, called by Antonio Gramsci 'political society' (*società politica*), but also as a constellation of institutions in civil society (*società civile*). Here, in civil society, the necessary consensus about the patterns of regulation and the shape of social relations has to be constantly (re)produced; otherwise, the governmental coercive apparatus will be in danger of destabilisation. For social work theory, the relevant point is that civil society in national and welfare states includes social work and education agencies. This is an often ignored fact in the English-speaking as well as international social work debates, clearly made here by Garrett: social work as a professional agency *is* part of the nation and welfare state. I would even go further and argue that social work is about the state not only because, 'by and large, social workers are employed by the state' , but also because it is always a 'task in public responsibility' (Hamburger, 2011, s 1035, own translation). Thus, where, when and whether social work is delivered is a 'public issue', decided, ultimately, by citizens.

Another often overlooked aspect in social work debates that Paul Michael Garrett calls our attention to in his considerations is the understanding of social work transformation as an ongoing process. While there were not always periods of transformation in history, especially not in the fundamental way that we are experiencing currently (something like this has probably only once been experienced in the history of professional social work: in the 19th century, when professional social work was implemented), so transformation cannot be seen as a shift away from some 'authentic or timeless form of practice'; its shape is and was always an object of political struggles. This leads us to a third point that we should learn from Paul Michael Garrett's considerations: social work debates have to be engaged in a 'political reading of social work', like the one Garrett himself offers us in his piece on social work with children and families in England and the Republic of Ireland. Also, social work theory and research, as well as social work practice, have to be clear about being part of that political struggle. There is a long tradition of thinking in social work as being colonised by social policy – or even criminal and health policy, and, in the present, by neoliberal agencies, such as 'the management' or a privatised sector. Social work is seen, then, as being part of or even on the side of the lifeworld of its users (see Pozzuto et al, 2006) . But, as Paul Michael Garrett makes clear, social work is not part of the lifeworld, but of the 'system' – in Habermas's words, of the state. Social work is and cannot be 'innocent', and its transformation is not only a result of 'outside' powers. Therefore, we have to be clear on

—

focusing on the agents of the current transformation, precisely also *in* the field of social work.

This insight brings us to the second undercurrent in Paul Michael Garrett's considerations: his interest is not only in presenting a piece of what we can call a critical analysis of the current transformation, which is at the moment dearly necessary (see also Rogowski, 2012a), but also in looking for a perspective to regain transformation as a critical and radical concept for social work. So, he is calling for an explicitly 'critical theory' (Max Horkheimer 1968 [1937]): that is, a theory – and research, we can add – that always aims to transform social reality, and not only analyse it. In the words of Paul Michael Garrett:

> Given this project [the 'neoliberal transformation], there is a need to create a different set of social and political possibilities founded on total opposition to a destabilised and vengeful capitalism. Here, the challenge is to create a European movement intent on building new alliances and to participate in actions that are intent on resisting capital's endeavour to remake and reorder the world. Specifically, in terms of social work, engaging in such oppositional activity is, of course, a far from easy task because those in positions of structural power (and invested with the power of naming and defining) seek to maintain hegemony and identify what is permissible and what should be 'closed down'.

However, as convincing as this call for alternatives is, there are two aspects, from my point of view, which we should work on a little further than Garrett's considerations bring us to. First, as academics in social work, the position you are writing from should make you aware of your own part in the game. That critical reflection is missing in Paul Michael Garrett's considerations: where is social work education standing at the moment due to the current transformation in England and the Republic of Ireland? What does it mean to work on a critical and radical perspective in social work research currently? Second, in a critical analysis, like the one Garrett offers us, the danger of claiming '"spaces" for a more critical engagement' by mentioning only those initiatives that label themselves explicitly as critical and/or radical can be a short cut and an underestimation of other subversive, resistant or denying practices – especially those going on in the practice of social work education, in everyday life delivery or on the organisational level in child and youth services (see Evans and Harris, 2004).

However, both aspects come with the perspective of a problematisation of the present – even Paul Michael Garrett never claims explicitly for that perspective. It is of absolute importance to name the hegemonic development lines (political rationalities), but, at the same time, such a critical analysis tends to be weak in being aware of what is going on in the contradictions of everyday life struggles.

Some concluding thoughts

Paul Michael Garrett

All the responses are erudite, knowledgeable and generous. All of the respondents are progressive thinkers with detailed understanding of developments relating to social work with children and families beyond my own base in the Republic of Ireland: England (Smith), Northern Ireland (Houston), Scotland (Woodward), Wales (Drakeford and Butler), elsewhere in Europe (Kessl, and Roets and Roose) and North America (Baines). It is, of course, impossible, to address all the issues raised in this short rejoinder, so the aim here is simply to address a handful of key points.

'Battlefield' notes

Some respondents imply that my perspective is rather gloomy, with Houston maintaining that there is a 'heavy sense of pessimism' emanating from my essay. More theoretically, according to Drakeford and Butler, my comprehension of hegemony may be too static and 'overdeterministic'. Moreover, serving to dilute my deployment of the Bourdieusian idea that the state is a 'battlefield', I seem to argue that the 'battle has already been concluded in favour of neoliberalisation'.

My focus was on England and the Republic of Ireland, and in these locations, social workers seeking to create more progressive possibilities face considerable obstacles. Following Stuart Hall (2011, pp 727–8), it is clear that no:

—

project achieves a position of permanent 'hegemony'. It is a process, not a state of being. No victories are final. Hegemony has constantly to be 'worked on', maintained, renewed and revised. Excluded social forces, whose consent has not been won, whose interests have not been taken into account, form the basis of countermovements, resistance, alternative strategies and visions … and the struggle over a hegemonic system starts anew.

Despite, the 'recurrent trope of collective pain' (Clarke and Newman, 2012, p 303), it is apparent that the ruling class has embarked on an offensive against the working class. In these circumstances, it seems important to try and arrive at an accurate assessment of the possibilities afforded for resistance and fightback.

A survey by the European Trade Union Institute has illuminated that there is considerable variation in the so-called financial 'adjustment' or 'austerity' packages across European countries (Theodoropoulou and Watt, 2011). To some extent, administrations in France and Iceland reveal that there are alternative and somewhat more socially benign ways to respond to the current crisis. However, in terms of the UK government, the 'planned spending cuts are greater and more sustained than those inflicted by the governments of Margaret Thatcher in the early 1980s' (Theodoropoulou and Watt, 2011, p 15). Hall (2011, p 707) has asserted that the 'welfare state made deep inroads into private capital's territory. To roll back that post-war "settlement" and restore the prerogatives of capital has been the ambition of its opponents ever since Churchill'. Thus, in England, we can observe what we might term 'posh-boy revanchism', intent on eradicating the gains accrued by working people during the years after the Second World War and into the late 1970s. This project is *intentionally* widening the cleavage between the very rich and the poor and further embedding processes of 'accumulation by dispossession' (Harvey, 2005). As Ruth Levitas (2012, p 327, emphasis in original) reports:

The *Sunday Times* Rich List for 2010 revealed an unprecedented rise in 2009 in the wealth of the richest 1000 individuals in

Britain – an increase of £77 billion, or about 30 per cent. Their combined wealth holdings then totalled over £335 billion, more than one-third of the national debt. Half of this was held by the richest 100 individuals. If we had merely taxed the 2009 *increase* in wealth for the top 1000 individuals at 50 per cent, it would have generated £38 billion – more than six times the immediate cuts imposed by the Coalition's Emergency Budget in 2010.

Those receiving social services are increasing ridiculed, denounced or demonised as welfare 'spongers' (Garthwaite, 2011) or potential perpetrators of child neglect. For example, 'early intervention' is central to the Coalition's rhetorical agenda for social work and associated professions (Allen and Smith, 2008; Casey, 2012; Centre for Social Justice, 2012). However, seemingly central to this discourse is contempt for poor and socially marginalised families. Furthermore, Michael Gove (2012) – the current Secretary of State for Education – is intent on modernising social work for the late 19th century and is aiming to situate child *rescue* as the core of the professional task:

> In all too many cases when we decide to leave children in need with their biological parents we are leaving them to endure a life of soiled nappies and scummy baths, chaos and hunger, hopelessness and despair. These children need to be rescued, just as much as the victims of any other natural disaster.

An emergent strand within this presentation of social work is the notion that elites should become proactive and influence the dispossessed and 'those with no professional aspirations' (Heawood, 2008, p 42). Detectable in the media after the death of Baby Peter Connelly (Heawood, 2008), this is now apparent in Gove's endorsement of the 'brilliant idea', promulgated by the Institute of Public Policy Research (IPPR), to alter the class composition of the social work workforce. The IPPR is concerned that, in 2011, only 6% of those beginning social work training came from the elite 'Russell Group' of universities. A mooted organisation, called 'Frontline', will therefore 'attract the *best people* into one of Britain's toughest professions. It will create an elite route into frontline children's social work' (MacAlister, 2012, p 24, emphasis added).

As for actual practice, and particularly with regards to concerns about the constraints posed by e-working (Garrett, 2005), the Munro Review suggested that there would be a new emphasis on building relationships with service users and less direction from the centre. Change in this direction would be very much welcomed (Broadhurst and Mason, 2012). However, given the government's more encompassing agenda for the profession – which aims to fracture local authority provision and to introduce a myriad of so-called 'independent' providers – it is hard to be confident about a progressive shift if the trajectory of social work in England is to be determined by the Conservative–Liberal Democrat Coalition.

A 'progressive universalism' beyond Westminster?

Post-devolution, it is clearly important to be attentive to the different emerging configurations and ways of trying to construct social work. However, Rona Woodward indicates that processes of intensified neoliberalisation impacting on social work in England are also to be found in Scotland despite the 'more collective ideology' informing Scottish policymaking (Scott and Wright, 2012, p 441):

> The Scottish Government continues to only partially govern the welfare state – with control over services (the care side), but without influence over benefits and employment services (the cash side), which have developed according to principles and priorities that are 'incongruent' with aspirations to forge a more progressive polity and one that might impact in a more beneficial way on social work with children and families. (Scott and Wright, 2012, p 448)

The argument for greater local control is complex and beyond the scope of this discussion. However, it is apparent that more local or regional control for the administration of social security in places such as Sweden has not necessarily resulted in better services (Scott and Wright, 2012).

Drakeford and Butler make a powerful case for Wales as the exception, proving that, they avow, it remains possible for traditional social-democratic politics to create 'a more sympathetic policy environment'. Apart from registering a warranted ambivalence about social work's 'radical' potential, their contribution has little to say about the profession; the focus is much more on the policy dimension. One of the writers is a Labour member of the National Assembly for Wales and chair of its Health and Social Services Committee, and the thrust of the argument appears to be that a form of 'progressive universalism' (Drakeford, 2012) can be safeguarded if there is sufficient resolve and pragmatism on the part of strategically located elected members. In this sense, it is implied, the debating chamber in Cardiff Bay can serve as a beacon to others hankering for a more progressive politics.

As in the Scottish case, it is argued that the more politically progressive bloc in Wales is better placed to try to alleviate the worst, most reactionary, aspects of the policies of the Westminster government. However – like in Scotland – it is easy to see how more progressive initiatives can be stalled or even reversed by the Westminster government. Important here, once again, is the central government's ability to introduce cuts that impinge on practitioners' work with children and families on a daily basis. As Drakeford (2012, p 463) concedes:

> the Emergency Budget of June 2010 introduced net cuts to the welfare system of £11 billion a year by 2015. The Comprehensive Spending Review of the following October added a further £7 billion reduction. Cumulatively, best estimates suggest that over £2 billion of these cuts will fall in Wales.

Clearly, cuts of this scale shrink the ability to forge more progressive possibilities.

The state as 'debt collector': the Republic of Ireland

Across the Irish Sea, the Republic of Ireland provides an example of the demise of the type of 'progressive universalism' led by the Labour Party and championed by Drakeford and Butler. Here, the Labour Party in government – as a minority partner with Fine Gael – is actively pursuing the neoliberal agenda. Paradoxically, the country could be:

> presented as a textbook case for the failures of neoliberalism.... Yet far from producing a re-think, the crash has led to an intensification of neoliberal policies. In fact, Ireland has led the way in Europe in promoting such a response. (Allen, 2012, p 425)

As Kieran Allen (2012, p 436) elaborates:

> In its endeavours to be the best pupil in the class, the Irish government has taken €24 billion out of its economy since 2008 in a series of five harsh budgets. That is the equivalent of 16 per cent of its GDP and represents the biggest fiscal adjustment of any advanced country in the past thirty years.... If GDP is the measure used, the Irish debt is scheduled to peak at 150 per cent by 2013 and even that is based on modest hopes of some growth. Should that occur – and it seems the most likely scenario – then Ireland will enter the same territory as Greece.

Indeed, Ireland presents the perfect illustration of Wolfgang Streeck's (2011, p 28) argument that formally democratic states are slowly 'being turned into debt-collecting agencies on behalf of a global oligarchy of investors' (see also United Nations General Assembly, 2011). Despite the duplicitous 'sharing the pain' rhetoric at the core of the Irish programme of cuts, the findings of the EU Inclusion Living Conditions survey, conducted in 2010 and published in March 2011, revealed that the disposable income of the poorest households fell by 18.6% in a single year, while the income of the richest rose by 4.1% (Social Justice Ireland, 2012). Unsurprising, this has promoted social suffering and has impacted on an array of social work concerns (see, eg, Mental Health Commission, 2011). It is estimated that approximately '20 per cent of households are now in significant debt, primarily through a combination of increases in mortgage payments (within a context of negative equity) and a significant loss of income (through unemployment and/or reductions in pay)' (Barry and Conroy, 2012, p 2). What is more, it is children who are:

> the most vulnerable to poverty in Ireland. In 2010, nearly one in five children was at risk of poverty and over 8% were living in consistent poverty, an increase of a third over the 2008 level. The reduction of the child benefit payment by 15 per cent in 2011 (on top of a 10 per cent cut in 2010) means a further increase in child poverty rates. (Barry and Conroy, 2012, p xx)

Where does social work stand in this conjuncture? After the publication of the Ryan Report (Commission to Inquire into Child Abuse, 2009), the previous government gave a commitment to create an additional 270 social work posts. However, practitioners within the sector argue that some of these posts were used to fill existing gaps in the service created as a result of previous employment embargos (Burns and MacCarthy, 2012, p 30). In terms of the more fundamental messages conveyed in the Ryan Report, there is ample evidence that children perceived as 'troublesome' are still being incarcerated in appalling conditions. This applies especially to the St Patrick's Institution in Dublin (Ombudsman for Children's Office, 2011; Office of the Inspector of Prisons, 2012). It is also reasonable to suggest that there is an incarcerative continuum involving those children compelled to remain in so-called 'direct provision' for asylum seekers (Arnold, 2012).

As noted in my original essay, the profession and the wider 'child and family services' terrain is the focus of a problematic 'change agenda' (Task Force on the Child and Family Support Agency, 2012). In this context, many have expressed concerns that the current government is moving towards overly rigid time limits for assessments and more e-working. Thus, there is a 'paradox that at a time where developments such as standardisation are under serious scrutiny in England, they are being embraced in Ireland' (Featherstone et al, 2012, p 49). Here, particular criticisms have been directed at the Business Process Standardisation Project (BPSP). As Featherstone and her colleagues observed, the Integrated Children's System (ICS) attempted to micro-manage practice and there are obvious similarities between the BPSP and the discredited ICS workflow model.

Given these circumstances, is there room for a more progressive politics within the children and families sector? Is there still the potential to try to create a counter-hegemony? Houston, for example, introduces productive ideas related to the occupational and discursive space, which may still be available to social workers. Before picking up on this idea and exploring its possibilities in more detail, it is important to refer to Fabian Kessl's remarks on academics in social work.

Our 'part in the game'

In his response, Kessl maintains that 'as academics in social work, the position you are writing from should make you aware of your own part in the game' and that this 'critical reflection is missing' from my considerations. I do, in fact, explicitly refer to this very dimension in my first endnote to the article. There is no attempt to render my location invisible or neutral. However, Kessl's point is pertinent and merits a little more elaboration. To be sure, the university is not the social work office and the social work office is not the university. The university social work programme and social work practice are connected but discrete and distinct locations and, despite both being moulded by processes of intensified neoliberalisation, those positioned within these two fields of operation are apt to view the world somewhat differently.

The sensory and affective nature of social work is unlike that found on the university campus; yet, this point is rarely mentioned in the literature on social work emanating from university-based writers pronouncing on the field of practice (see also Garrett, 2013, p 1). As Althusser (2011 [1964]) observed in the early 1960s, the university is in a special and privileged position in relation to the social division of labour. This still holds true for academic staff with full-time contracts, but might not be as true for more precariously placed academics, and even less so for others working within the university 'community', for example, as cleaners.

It might be suggested that academics connected to social work and student placements are less likely to inhabit an entirely 'scholastic disposition' (Bourdieu, 2000) and more likely to be attuned to the practical concerns of the world than those located in less applied disciplines. Nevertheless, for those of us working in an academic field, there is still more autonomy, at various levels, than for practitioners. Here, Rancière's comments from the early 1970s remain pertinent. He argued that the bourgeoisie in the industrial West reserved particular types of freedom for intellectuals: the 'freedom to say anything and everything at the university, where intellectuals can be Marxists, Leninists, even Maoists, provided *they perpetuate its functioning*' (Rancière, 2011 [1974], p 112, emphasis added). Kessl implies that such an understanding might aid academics in social work fathom, as Rancière encourages, the 'real power relations' wherein our own theoretical discourse is produced. This entails interrogating the 'place where this discourse is produced' and then going on to 'inscribe this discourse in a practice directed at transforming' power relations in and beyond the precincts of the university (Rancière, 2011 [1974], p 114). What possibilities, therefore, might be available for creating transforming strategies?

Is another social work is possible?

Donna Baines, based in Canada, rightly cautions that 'much of social work is not and never was about social justice or fairness'. If this is so, it could be argued that 'radicalism' might better be relocated to more overtly political activity within leftist parties and trade unions. The problem with this analysis, if pushed to its limits, is that it can extinguish the very idea of radical praxis *within* the field of social work.

The Social Work Action Network (SWAN), present now in England, Scotland, Wales, the Republic of Ireland, Canada, South

Africa, Hong Kong and Australia, may have a key role to play. Kindred organisations in Belguim and Germany may be fulfilling similar roles. Importantly, if they are allowed to *breathe* and remain free from the domination of a single political party, such groups may have the potential to create a freer space beyond the social work office and the university. Central to the SWAN agenda is the notion that new resources of hope and political vibrancy are to be found in the growth of users' movements (such as the disability movement and the mental health users movement), which have brought innovation and insight to our ways of seeing social and individual problems. This perspective has particular resonance in Ireland, where those incarcerated in Industrial Schools and similar institutions, such as the Magdalen Laundries, have self-organised and campaigned for public inquiries into how they were treated. Similarly, in recent months, it has been people with disabilities leading opposition against benefit cuts. Such initiatives illuminate the potentiality of self-organised collective movements. The debates they spark can also 'help us think about the shape of an ... engaged social work based around such core "anti-capitalist" values as democracy, solidarity, accountability, participation, justice, equality, liberty and diversity' (Jones et al, 2004).

SWAN is:

> a radical, campaigning organisation of social work and social care practitioners, students, service users, carers and academics, united by our concern that social work practice is being undermined by managerialism and marketisation, by the stigmatisation of service users and by welfare cuts and restrictions. (Jones et al, 2004)

Here is not the place to dwell on the history and focal aims and objectives of the organisation (see, eg, Lavalette, 2011a). Rather, I will conclude by focusing on the local, and the micro, to hint at what a radical social work may look like in a particular place – Galway in the west of Ireland.

How might a local SWAN section try to be different? How might its espoused 'radicalism' be reflected in its internal structure and modalities of operation? First, reflecting some of the discussions taking place in Galway, SWAN might strive to be a community of equality, seeking to create a flat, non-hierarchical space in which practitioners, students, service users and academics can congregate to think, to plan and to act. Second, related to this, each local section should operate democratically and promote diligent organisational and administrative practices. Third, a local section of SWAN should seek to be a 'leftist' voice committed to challenging the 'primary definers' of the role of social workers. This would involve, following Houston's comments, an aspiration to try to *occupy* the discursive ground and not be destabilised if chided for being 'too political' or – more patronisingly – naive. Fourth would be the need to construct a counter-hegemony: to think differently, do things differently and to seek to organise a new 'common sense' within and beyond social work, which strives to put people before profit. This involves connecting to other groups and building coalitions with sometimes seemingly entirely different interests. Fifth, there is the need to recognise the importance of working in trade unions. Public sector unions in Ireland are frequently pilloried in the media, even blamed for creating the economic crisis. However, SWAN is not an alternative to trade unions and it is vital to work within unions. This is also connected to the idea that it is foolish to act singularly – the aim must be to prompt collective action and not to create valiant 'martyrs'. Sixth, despite the focus on the local/micro, there should also be an awareness of the national and international – the 'bigger picture'. At the same time, there has to be attentiveness to local conditions and circumstances.

There is, of course, a fusing at times of the organisational and the political thematic. In Ireland, the local SWAN section tentatively began to explore the notion that there are at least six key areas for future activity:

1. a focus on class politics and the role of the State (see also Garrett, 2012);
2. alertness to issues rooted in patriarchy and racialisation;

3. total opposition to neoliberal 'common sense' within social work practice and education in Ireland;

4. highlighting the fact that children who are poor or financially precarious are in this situation because of avoidable political and economic decisions;

5. a focus on children who are confined or subjected to other forms of restriction; and

6. a willingness to promote a new 'shop floor' social work politics opposing the deterioration of working practices and a further erosion of services.

These constitute, therefore, merely some of the ways in which social workers and others in the west of Ireland are seeking to confront, albeit in often small and seemingly mundane ways, the intensification of neoliberalisation. The 'battle' is not over.

References

Allen, G. and Duncan Smith, I. (2008) *Early intervention: good parents, great kids, better citizens*, London: Centre for Social Justice and the Smith Institute.

Allen, K. (2012) 'The model pupil who faked the test: social policy in the Irish crisis', *Critical Social Policy*, vol 32, no 3, pp 422–40.

Althusser, L. (2011 [1964]) 'Student problems', *Radical Philosophy*, vol 170, pp 11–16.

Apostel, L. (1985) 'Paradoxes in social work: a war on three fronts', in Seminar and Laboratory for youth welfare and adult education (eds) *The right to intervene: contributions to a seminar with reference to the superannuation of Prof Dr G. De Bock*. Antwerp: De Sikkel.

Arnold, S. (2012) *State sanctioned child poverty and exclusion: the case of children in state accommodation for asylum seekers*, Dublin: Irish Refugee Council.

Audit Commission (2008) 'Every child matters – are we there yet?', Press release, 29 October.

Bailey, B. and Brake, M. (1975) 'Introduction: social work in the welfare state', in B. Bailey and M. Brake (eds) *Radical social work*, New York, NY: Pantheon Books.

Baines, D. (2004a) 'Caring for nothing: work organization and unwaged labour in social services', *Work, Employment and Society*, vol 18, no 2, pp 267–95.

Baines, D. (2004b) 'Pro-market, non-market: the dual nature of organizational change in social services delivery', *Critical Social Policy*, vol 24, no 1, pp 5–29.

Baines, D. (2010) '"If we don't get back to where we were before": working in the restructured nonprofit social services', *British Journal of Social Work*, vol 40, no 3, pp 928-45.

Baines, D. (2011) 'An overview of anti-oppressive practice: roots, theory, tensions', in D. Baines (ed) *Doing anti-oppressive practice. Building transformative, politicized social work*, 2nd edn, Halifax: Fernwood Books, pp 2–24.

Baines, D. and Cunningham, I. (2011) 'Using comparative perspective rapid ethnography in international case studies: strengths and challenges', *Qualitative Social Work*, vel 12, no 1, pp 73–88.

Baines, D., Cunningham, I. and Fraser, H. (2011) 'Constrained by managerialism: caring as participation in the voluntary social services', *Economic and Industrial Democracy*, vol 32, no 2, pp 329–52.

Barnardos (2010) *Dreading December 2010*, Dublin: Barnardos.

Barry, U. and Conroy, P. (2012) 'Ireland 2008–2012: untold story of the crisis – gender, equality and inequalities'. Available at: http://www.tascnet.ie/upload/file/MurphyGenderGovernance.pdf

Bates, M. (2011) 'Evidence-based practice and anti-oppressive', in D. Baines (ed) *Doing anti-oppressive practice. Building transformative, politicized social work*, Halifax: Fernwood Books, pp 146–59.

Batty, E., Cole, I. and Green, S. (2011) *Low income neighbourhoods in Britain: the gap between policy ideas and residents' realities*, York: Joseph Rowntree Foundation.

BBC (British Broadcasting Corporation) (2011) 'England riots: broken society is top priority – Cameron', BBC News, 15 August.

Bellamy Foster, J. (1998) 'Introduction', in H. Braverman (ed) *Labour and monopoly capitalism: the degradation of work in the twentieth century – 25th anniversary edition*, New York, NY: Monthly Review Press, pp ix–xxv.

Beresford, P. and Hasler, F. (2009) *Transforming social care: changing the future together*, Uxbridge: Brunel University Centre for Citizen Participation.

Bieler, A. and Morton, A. (2003) 'Globalisation, the state and class struggle: a "Critical Economy" engagement with Open Marxism', *British Journal of Politics and International Relations*, vol 5, no 4, pp 467–99.

Blackstock, C., with Wallis, M.A. and Sunseri, L. (2010) *Colonialism and racism in Canada: historical traces and contemporary issues*, Toronto: Nelson Education Ltd.

Blackstock, C. and Trocme, N. (2005) 'Community-based child welfare for Aborginal children: supporting resilience through structural change', *Social Policy Journal of New Zealand*, vol 24 (March), pp 12–33.

Blond, P. (2010) *Red Tory*, London: Faber and Faber.

Boltanski, L. and Chiapello, E. (2005) *The new spirit of capitalism*, London: Verso.

Bone, J.D. (2012) 'The neoliberal phoenix: the Big Society or business as usual', *Sociological Research Online*, vol 17, no 2, p 16. Available at: http://www.socresonline.org.uk/17/2/16.html

Bonnar, S. (2010) *Report for the Mental Health Commission on admission of young people to adult mental health wards in the Republic of Ireland*, Dublin, Mental Health Commission. Available at: http://www.drugsandalcohol.ie/14501/1/MH_Comm_Report_on_Admission_of_Young_People_to_Adult_MH_Wards.pdf.

Bourdieu, P. (1991) *Language and symbolic power*, Boston: Harvard University Press.

Bourdieu, P. (2000) *Pascalian meditations*, Cambridge: Polity.

Bourdieu, P. (2001) *Acts of resistance: against the new myths of our time*, Cambridge: Polity.

Bourdieu, P. and Wacquant, L. (2001) 'NewLiberalSpeak: notes on the new planetary vulgate', *Radical Philosophy*, vol 105, pp 2–6.

Bouverne-De Bie, M., Impens, J., Willems, S., De Visscher, S., Delens-Ravier, I. and Rosseel, Y. (2011) *Een link tussen leven in armoede en maatregelen bijzondere jeugdbijstand?*, Gent: Academia Press.

Brake, M. and Bailey, B. (1980) 'Contributions to a Radical Practice in Social Work', in M. Brake and R. Bailey (eds) *Radical social work and practice*, London Edward Arnold.

Broadhurst, K. and Mason, C. (2012) 'Social work beyond the VDU: foregrounding co-presence in situated practice – why face-to-face practice matters', *British Journal of Social Work*, advanced electronic access from 5 September.

Brody, S. (2007) 'Readers' opinions: our 2007 poll results', *Community Care*, 13 December. Available at: http://www.communitycare.co.uk/articles/13/12/2007/106765/readers-opinions-our-2007-poll-results.htm.

Burke, M. (2011) 'Who benefits from the crisis in Ireland?', *Soundings*, vol 47, pp 130–47.

Burns, K. (2008) 'Making a difference: exploring job retention issues in child protection and welfare social work', in K. Burns and D. Lynch (eds) *Child protection and welfare social workers: contemporary themes and practice perspectives*, Dublin: Farmar, pp 60–75.

Burns, K. and Lynch, D. (eds) (2008) *Child protection and welfare social work*, Dublin: Farmar.

Burns, K. and MacCarthy, J. (2012) 'An impossible task? Implementing the recommendations of child abuse inquiry reports in a context of high workloads in child protection', *Irish Journal of Social Studies*, vol 12, no 1, pp 25–37.

Butler, I. (2011) 'Children's policy', in C. Williamson (ed) *New directions in social policy: social work/social welfare in a devolved Wales*, 2nd edn, Glasgow: Kelvin Books.

Butler, I. and Drakeford, M. (2005a) *Scandal, social policy and social welfare* 2nd revised edn, Bristol: The Policy Press/BASW.

Butler, I. and Drakeford, M. (2005b) 'Trusting in social work', *British Journal of Social Work*, vol 35, pp 639–54.

Butler, I. and Drakeford, M. (2010) 'Children and young people's policy in Wales', in P. Ayre and M. Preston-Shoot (eds) *Children's services at the crossroads: a critical evaluation of contemporary policy for practice*, Lyme Regis: Russell House.

Butler, I. and Drakeford, M. (2011) *Social work on trial: the Colwell Inquiry and the state of welfare*, Bristol: The Policy Press.

Butler, I. and Drakeford, M. (2012) *Social work on trial: the Colwell Inquiry and the state of welfare,* 2nd edn, Bristol: The Policy Press.

Butler, I. and Pugh, R. (2004) 'The politics of social work research', in R. Lovelock and J. Powell (eds) *Reflecting on social work - discipline and profession*, Aldershot: Ashgate.

Cabinet Office (2010a) 'Prime Minister launches the Big Society Bank and announces the first four big society communities', Press notice, 19 July. Available at: https://www.gov.uk/government/news/prime-minister-launches-the-big-society-bank

Cabinet Office (2010b) 'Deputy Prime Minister to champion social mobility', Press notice, 18 August. Available at: https://www.gov.uk/government/news/deputy-prime-minister-to-champion-social-mobility

Cameron, D. (2010) 'Together in the national interest', speech to the Conservative Party Conference, 6 October.

Campaign 2000 (2012) 'End child and family poverty in Canada'. Available at: http://www.campaign2000.ca/reportCards/national/2011EnglishRreportCard.pdf

Camus, A. (1991 [1955]) *The myth of Sisyphus and other essays*, London: Vintage International.

Canadian Association of Schools of Social Work (2012) 'Standards for accreditation'. Available at: http://caswe-acfts.ca/wp-content/uploads/2013/03/COAStandardsMay2012.pdf

Cantillon, B. (2011) 'The paradox of the social investment state: growth, employment and poverty in the Lisbon era', *Journal of European Social Policy*, vol 21, no 5, pp 432–49.

Cardy, S. (2011) '"Care matters" and the privatization of looked after children's services in England and Wales: developing a critique of independent "social work practices"', *Critical Social Policy*, vol 31, no 4, pp 430–42.

Care Standards Tribunal (2008) *LA v General Social Care Council*.

Carey, M. (2009) 'It's a bit like being a robot or working in a factory', *Organization*, vol 16, no 4, pp 505–27.

Carniol, B. (2010) *Case critical: the dilemma of social work in Canada,* 6th edn, Toronto: Between the Lines.

Casey, L. (2012) 'Listening to troubled families', Department for Communities and Local Government. Available at: https://www.gov.uk/government/uploads/system/uploads/attachment_data/file/6151/2183663.pdf

Castle, B. (1980) *The Castle diaries 1974–76*, London: Weidenfeld and Nicolson.

Centre for Social Justice (2012) *Rethinking child poverty*, London: Centre for Social Justice.

Chief Secretary to the Treasury (2003) *Every child matters*, Cm 5860, London: HMSO. Available at: https://www.education.gov.uk/consultations/downloadableDocs/EveryChildMatters.pdf

ChildStats.gov (2011) 'America's children: key national indicators of well-being'. Available at: http://www.childstats.gov/americaschildren/index3.asp.

Clarke, J. and Newman, J. (2012) 'The alchemy of austerity', *Critical Social Policy*, vol 32, no 3, pp 299–320.

Clarke, J., Newman, J., Smith, N., Vidler, E. and Westmarland, L. (2007) *Creating citizen-consumers: changing publics and changing public services*, London: Sage.

Commission of Investigation (2009) *Report into the Catholic Archdiocese of Dublin*, Dublin: Department of Justice, Equality and Law Reform.

Commission of Investigation (2010) *Report into the Catholic Diocese of Cloyne*, Dublin: Department of Justice, Equality and Law Reform.

Commission to Inquire into Child Abuse (2009) *Commission to Inquire into Child Abuse report*, Dublin: Stationery Office.

Conservative Party Commission on Social Workers (2007) *No more blame game – the future for children's social workers*, London, The Conservative Party. Available at: http://www.conservatives.com/~/media/Files/Downloadable%20Files/No%20More%20Blame%20Game.ashx?dl=true%20-%202008-09-12.

Daniel, B., Burgess, C. and Scott, J. (2012) *Review of child neglect in Scotland*, Edinburgh: Action for Children/Scottish Government.

Davies, N. and Williams, D. (2009) *Clear red water: Welsh devolution and socialist politics*, London: Francis Boutle Publishers.

Department of Education (2010) 'Review of child protection: better frontline services to protect children', Press notice, 10 June.

Department of Education (2011) *The Munro review of child protection: final report*, London: TSO.

Department of Health and Children (1999) *Children first: national guidelines for the protection and welfare of children*, Dublin: Stationery Office.

DfE (Department for Education) (2011) *A new approach to child poverty: tackling the causes of disadvantage and transforming families' lives*, London: Department for Education.

Dolan, P. (2010) 'Intensive family supports can aid detection of abuse', *The Irish Times*, 29 October, p 16.

Dorling, D. and Thomas, B. (2011) *Bankrupt Britain: an atlas of social change*, Bristol: The Policy Press.

Drakeford, M. (2007a) 'Governance and social policy', in C. Williams (ed) *Social policy for social welfare practice in a devolved Wales*, Birmingham: Venture Press.

Drakeford, M. (2007b) 'Progressive universalism', *Agenda* (Institute of Welsh Affairs), winter, pp 4–7.

Drakeford, M. (2010) 'Devolution and youth justice in Wales', *Criminology and Criminal Justice*, vol 10, no 2, pp 137–54.

Drakeford, M. (2012) 'Wales in the age of austerity', *Critical Social Policy*, vol 32, no 3, pp 454–67.

Duncan, S. (2007) 'What's the problem with teenage parents? And what's the problem with policy?', *Critical Social Policy*, vol 27, no 3, pp 307–34.

Elliott, L. (2010) 'A brand of austerity about as progressive as Thatcher's', *The Guardian*, 26 August, p 30.

Evans, T. and Harris, J. (2004) 'Street-level bureaucracy, social work and the (exaggerated) death of discretion', *British Journal of Social Work*, vol 34, no 6, pp 871–95.

Family Champion Employment Guide (2007) *Working families everywhere*. Available at: http://www.familyandparenting.org/our_work/Parenting/Working+Families

Fargion, S. (2012) 'Synergies and tensions in child protection and parent support: policy lines and practitioners' cultures', *Child and Family Social Work*, published online, May. Available at: http://onlinelibrary.wiley.com/doi/10.1111/j.1365-2206.2012.00877.x/pdf

Featherstone, B., White, S. and Wastell, D. (2012) 'Ireland's opportunity to learn from England's difficulties? Auditing uncertainty in child protection', *Irish Journal of Applied Social Studies*, vol 12, no 1, pp 49–62.

Ferguson, H. (2001) 'Social work, individualization and life politics', *British Journal of Social Work*, vol 31, no 1, pp 41–55.

Ferguson, H. (2004) *Protecting children in time: child abuse, child protection and the consequences of modernity*, Houndmills: Palgrave Macmillan.

Ferguson, H. (2011) *Child protection practice*, Houndmills: Palgrave Macmillan.

Ferguson, I. and Woodward, R. (2009) *Radical social work in practice*, Bristol: The Policy Press.

Finlayson, A. (2010) 'The broken society versus the social recession', *Soundings*, vol 44, pp 22–35.

Finn, D. (2011) 'Ireland on the turn?', *New Left Review*, vol 67, pp 5–41.

Foucault, M. (1979) *Discipline and punish: the birth of the prison*, New York, NY: Vintage Books.

Foucault, M. (1988) 'The art of telling the truth', in M. Foucault (ed) *Politics, philosophy, culture. Interviews and writings 1977–1984*, London: Routledge, pp 86–95.

Fraser, N. (2010) *Scales of justice: Reimagining political space in a globalizing world*, New York, NY: Columbia University Press.

Freeman, B. (2011) 'Indigenous pathways to anti-oppressive practice', in D. Baines (ed) *Doing anti-oppressive practice. Building transformative, politicized social work*, 2nd edn, Halifax: Fernwood Books, pp 116–32.

Galabuzzi, G. (2006) *Canada's economic apartheid: the social exclusion of racialized groups in the new century*, Toronto: Canadian Scholars Press Inc.

Gallagher, M. (2010) *Engaging with involuntary service users. Literature review 2: children and families*, Edinburgh: University of Edinburgh.

Gardiner, H. (2007) *Five minds for the future*, Boston, MA: Harvard Business School Press.

Garrett, P.M. (2003) *Remaking social work with children and families: a critical discussion on the 'modernisation' of social care*, London: Routledge.

Garrett, P.M. (2005) 'Social work's "electronic turn": notes on the deployment of information and communication technologies in social work with children and families', *Critical Social Policy*, vol 25, no 4, pp 529–54.

Garrett, P.M. (2009) *'Transforming' children's services? Social work, neoliberalism and the 'modern' world*, Maidenhead: Open University Press.

Garrett, P.M. (2012) 'Adjusting "our notions of the nature of the state": a political reading of Ireland's child protection crisis', *Capital & Class*, vol 36, no 2, pp 263–81.

Garrett, P.M. (2013) *Social work and social theory*, Bristol: The Policy Press.

Garthwaite, K. (2011) 'The language of shirkers and scroungers?', *Disability & Society*, vol 26, no 3, pp 369–72.

Gibbons, N. (2010) 'Roscommon child care case: report of the inquiry team to the Health Service Executive'. Available at: http://www.hse.ie/eng/services/Publications/services/Children/RoscommonChildCareCase.pdf

Giddens, A. (1998) *The third way: the renewal of social democracy*, Cambridge: Polity Press.

Giroux, H. (2012) *Twilight of the social: resurgent publics in the age of disposability*, New York, NY: Paradigm.

Gove, M. (2012) 'The failure of child protection and the need for a fresh start', 16 November. Available at: http://www.education.gov.uk/inthenews/speeches/a00217075/gove-speech-on-child-protection

Grass, G. and Bourdieu, P. (2002 [1999]) 'The "progressive" restoration', *The New Left Review*, vol 14, March–April. Available at: http://newleftreview.org/II/14/pierre-bourdieu-gunter-grass-the-progressive-restoration (accessed 23 June 2012).

Hall, S. (2003) 'New Labour's double-shuffle', *Soundings*, vol 24, pp 10–25.

Hall, S. (2011) 'The neo-liberal revolution', *Cultural Studies*, vol 25, no 6, pp 705–28.

Hamburger, F. (2011) 'Öffentlichkeit(en)', in H.-U. Otto and H. Thiersch (eds) *Handbuch Soziale Arbeit*, München: Reinhardt, pp 1030–6.

Harris, J. (2003) *The social work business*, London: Routledge.

Harvey, D. (2005) *A brief history of neoliberalism*, Oxford: Oxford University Press.

Healy, K. and Darlington, Y. (2009) 'Service user participation in diverse child protection contexts: principles for practice', *Child and Family Social Work*, vol 14, no 4, pp 420–30.

Heawood, S. (2008) 'The world around Baby P is wrong, why are we afraid to say so?', *The Independent on Sunday*, 16 November, pp 42–3.

Hendrick, H. (1994) *Child welfare England 1872–1989*, London: Routledge.

Hertmans, S. (2011) 'Politics is caught in a dream', *De Morgen*, 31 December.

Hills, J. and Stewart, K. (2005) *Policies towards poverty, inequality and exclusion since 1997*, York: Joseph Rowntree Foundation.

HIQA (Health Information and Quality Authority) (2010a) 'Ballydowd Special Care Unit' (Inspection Report 410), 31 August.

HIQA (2010b) 'Coovagh House Special Care Unit' (Inspection Report 590), 15 December.

HIQA (2010c) 'Gleann Alainn Special Care Unit' (Inspection Report 589), 15 December.

Hobsbawm, E. (2008) 'The £500bn question', *The Guardian*, 9 October, p 28.

Holohan, C. (2011) *In plain sight: responding to the Ferns, Ryan, Murphy and Cloyne Reports*, Dublin: Amnesty International Ireland.

Horkheimer, M. (1968 [1937]) 'Traditionelle und kritische Theorie', in M. Horkheimer (ed) *Kritische Theorie, Band 2*, Frankfurt a.M: Springer VS, pp 137-200.

Hothersall, S.J. and Walker, P. (2010) 'Children and their families', in S.J. Hothersall and J. Bolger (eds) *Social policy for social work, social care and the caring professions: Scottish perspectives*, Farnham: Ashgate.

Irish Prison Chaplains (2010) *The Irish Chaplains' annual report*. Available at: http://www.catholicbishops.ie/2010/11/29/irish-prison-chaplains-annual-report-2010/

Jones, C. (2001) 'Voices from the front line: state social workers and New Labour', *British Journal of Social Work*, vol 31, no 4, pp 547–62.

Jones, C. (2009) 'The myths of child protection', in I. Ferguson and M. Lavalette (eds) *Social work after Baby P: issues, debates and alternative perspectives*, Liverpool: Liverpool Hope University.

Jones, C., Ferguson, I., Lavalette, M. and Penketh, L. (2004) *Social work and social justice: a manifesto for a new engaged practice*. Available at: http://www.socialworkfuture.org/about-swan/national-organisation/manifesto.

JRF (Joseph Rowntree Foundation) (2010) *Monitoring poverty and social exclusion in Scotland, findings*, London: Joseph Rowntree Foundation.

Kearney, N. and Skehill, C. (ed) (2005) *Social work in Ireland: historical perspectives*, Dublin: Institute of Public Administration.

Keil, R. (2009) 'The urban politics of roll-with-it neoliberalization', *City*, vol 13, nos 2/3, pp 231–46.

Kemp, T. (2008) 'Questioning quality: a critical analysis of the development and implementation of the "quality agenda" and its impact on child protection social work practice in Ireland', in K. Burns and D. Lynch (eds) *Child protection and welfare social workers: contemporary themes and practice perspectives*, Dublin: A & A Farmar, pp 97–110.

Klein, N. (2007) *The shock doctrine: the rise of disaster capitalism*, London: Allen Lane.

Kulchyski, P., McCaskill, D. and Newhouse, B. (eds) (1999) *In the words of the elders: Aboriginal cultures in transition*, Toronto: University of Toronto Press.

Lavalette, M. (2011a) 'Introduction', in M. Lavalette (ed) *Radical social work today: social work at the crossroads*, Bristol: The Policy Press.

Lavalette, M. (ed) (2011b) *Radical social work today: social work at the crossroads*, Bristol: The Policy Press.

Leach, J. and Hanton, A. (2012) *Intergenerational Fairness Index: measuring changes in intergenerational fairness in the United Kingdom*, London: Intergenerational Foundation.

Le Grand, J. (2007) *Consistent care matters: exploring the potential of social work practices*, London: Department for Education and Skills.

Lero, D. and Kyle, L. (1991) 'Work, families and children in Ontario', in L. Johnson and D. Barnhorst (eds) *Children, families and public policy in the 90s*, Toronto: Thompson Educational Publishing.

Levitas, R. (2012) 'The just's umbrella: austerity and the Big Society in Coalition policy and beyond', *Critical Social Policy*, vol 32, no 3, pp 320–43.

Lorenz, W. (2008) 'Paradigms and politics: understanding methods paradigms in an historical context: the case of social pedagogy', *British Journal of Social Work*, vol 38, no 4, pp 625–44.

Lundy, C. (2011) *Social work, social justice and human rights. A structural approach to practice*, Toronto: University of Toronto Press.

Lunny, L., McHugh, J. and Brosnan, K. (2008) 'Monageer inquiry'. Available at: http://www.omc.gov.ie/documents/child_welfare_protection/MonageerReport.pdf

Lymbery, M. (2011) 'Social work at the crossroads', *British Journal of Social Work*, vol 31, no 3, pp 369–84.

MacAlister, J. (ed) (2012) *Frontline: improving the children's social work profession*, London: IPPR.

Mackay, K. and Woodward, R. (2010) 'Exploring the place of values in the new social work degree in Scotland', *Social Work Education*, vol 29, no 6, pp 633–45.

Marquand, D. (2008) 'The progressive consensus: hope for the future or fight to the past?', in J. Osmond (ed) *Unpacking the progressive consensus*, Cardiff: Cardiff University and the Institute of Welsh Affairs

Marston, G. and McDonald, C. (2012) 'Getting beyond "heroic agency" in conceptualizing social workers as policy actors in the twenty-first century', *British Journal of Social Work*, advanced access.

McDonald, C. (2006) *Challenging social work: the institutional context of practice*, Basingstoke: Palgrave Macmillan.

McGhee, J. and Waterhouse, L. (2011) 'Locked out of prevention? The identity of child and family-oriented social work in Scottish post-devolution policy', *British Journal of Social Work*, vol 41, no 6, pp 1088–104.

McKendrick, J., Mooney, G., Dickie, J. and Kelly, P. (eds) (2011) *Poverty in Scotland 2011: towards a more equal Scotland*, London: Child Poverty Action Group.

McLaughlin, K. (2007) 'Regulation and risk in social work: the General Social Care Council and the Social Care Register in context', *British Journal of Social Work*, vol 37, no 2, pp 1263–77.

McLaughlin, K. (2010) 'The social worker versus the General Social Care Council: an analysis of care standards tribunal hearings and decisions', *British Journal of Social Work*, vol 40, no 1, pp 311–27.

Mental Health Commission (2011) 'The human cost: an overview of the evidence on economic adversity and mental health and recommendations for action'. Available at: http://www.mhcirl.ie/File/HCPaper.pdf

Merrill Lynch and Capgemini (2011) 'Merrill Lynch Global Wealth Management and Capgemini release 15th annual World Wealth Report', Press release, 22 June.

Mooney, G. (2011) 'Poverty and anti-poverty policy in Scotland: themes and issues', in J.H. McKendrick, G. Mooney, J. Dickie and P. Kelly (eds) *Poverty in Scotland 2011: towards a more equal Scotland*, London: Child Poverty Action Group.

Mooney, G. and Scott, G. (2012) 'Devolution, social justice and social policy: the Scottish context', in G. Mooney and G. Scott (eds) *Social justice and social policy in Scotland*, Bristol: The Policy Press.

Morgan, R. (2002) 'National Centre for Public Policy annual lecture', Swansea, University of Wales.

Murphy, F.D., Buckley, H. and Joyce, L. (2005) *The Ferns report*, Dublin: Stationery Office.

Nikoloski, Z. (2011) 'Impact of financial crisis on poverty in the developing world: an empirical approach', *Journal of Development Studies*, vol 47, no 11, pp 1757–79.

Nixon, J., Hunter, C., Parr, S., Myers, S., Whittle, S. and Sanderson, D. (2006) *Interim evaluation of rehabilitation projects for families at risk of losing their homes as a result of anti-social behaviour*, London: Office of the Deputy Prime Minister.

Norman, J. (2010) *The Big Society*, Buckingham: UBP.

NSPCC (National Society for the Prevention of Cruelty to Children) (2008) *Poverty and child maltreatment*, London: NSPCC inform.

NSWQB (National Social Work Qualification Board) (2006) *Social work posts in Ireland*, Dublin: NSWQB.

Office of the Inspector of Prisons (2012) *Report of an inspection of St. Patrick's Institution by the Inspector of Prisons Judge Michael Reilly*, Nenagh: Office of the Inspector of Prisons.

Office of the Minister for Children and Youth Affairs (2008) *National review of compliance with Children First: national guidelines for the protection and welfare of children*, Dublin: Stationery Office.

Ofsted, Healthcare Commission and HM Inspectorate of Constabulary (2008) *Joint area review: Haringey children's services authority area*, Houndmills: Palgrave Macmillan.

Ombudsman for Children's Office (2011) *Young people in St. Patrick's Institution*, Dublin: Ombudsman for Children's Office.

O'Toole, F. (2009) 'Lessons in the power of the Church', *The Irish Times Weekend Review*, 6 June, p 3.

Panitch, L. (1994) 'Globalisation and the state', in R. Miliband and L. Panitch (eds) *The Socialist Register*, vol 30. Available at: http://socialistregister.com/index.php/srv/article/view/5637#. Uk7N8d5wbGg

Parton, N. (2000) 'Some thoughts on the relationship between theory and practice in and for social work', *British Journal of Social Work*, vol 30, pp 449–63.

Parton, N. and O'Byrne, P. (2000) *Constructive social work*, London: Macmillan.

Pearson, G. (1975) *The deviant imagination*, London: Macmillan.

Peck, J. (2004) 'Geography and public policy: constructions of neoliberalism', *Progress in Human Geography*, vol 28, no 3, pp 392–405.

Peck, J. (2010) *Constructions of neoliberal reason*, Oxford: Oxford University.

Penketh, L. (2009) 'Too much pessimism?', in I. Ferguson and M. Lavalette (eds) *Social work after Baby P: issues, debates and alternative perspectives*, Liverpool: Liverpool Hope University.

Pozzuto, R., Dezendorf, P. and Arnd-Caddigan, M. (2006) 'Social work and the colonization of the life-world', *Critical Social Work*, vol 7, no 2. Available at: www.uwindsor.ca/criticalsocialwork/social-work-and-the-colonization-of-the-life-world (accessed 24 June 2012).

Raasch-Gilman, R. (2012) 'Occupying the movement action plan'. Available at: http://www.trainingforchange.org/node/724 (accessed 20 May 2102).

Raftery, M. (2009) 'Bishops lied and covered up', *The Irish Times*, 27 November, p 20.

Rancière, J. (2011 [1974]) *Althusser's lesson*, London: Continuum.

Reader, J. (1999) *Africa: a biography of the continent*, New York, NY: Vintage Books, Random House.

Report of a Committee of Inquiry (1996) *Kelly – a child is dead*, Dublin: Houses of the Oireachtas.

Reynaert, D. (2012) 'Children's rights education as a social work practice. An analysis of the meaning of the children's rights movement in implementing the UN Convention on the Rights of the Child', PhD dissertation, Ghent University.

Rogowski, S. (2012a) 'Social work with children and families: challenges and possibilities in the neo-liberal world', *British Journal of Social Work*, vol 42, no 5, pp 921–40.

Rogowski, S. (2012b) *Social work. The rise and fall of a profession?*, Bristol: The Policy Press.

Rojek, C., Peacock, G. and Collins, C. (1988) *Social work and received ideas*, Oxford: Routledge.

Roose, R., Roets, G. and Bouverne-De Bie, M. (2011) 'Irony and social work: in search of the happy Sisyphus', *British Journal of Social Work*, advanced access.

Roose, R., Roets, G. and Schiettecat, T. (forthcoming [a]) 'Implementing a strengths perspective in child welfare and protection: a challenge not to be taken lightly', *European Journal of Social Work*.

Roose, R., Roets, G., Van Houte, S., Vandenhole, W. and Reynaert, D. (forthcoming [b]) 'From parental engagement to the engagement of social work services: discussing reductionist and democratic forms of partnership with families', *Child & Family Social Work*.

Ross, M. (2011) 'Social work activism amidst neoliberalism: a big, broad tent of activism' in D. Baines (ed), *Doing anti-oppressive practice: social justice social work*, Halifax/Winnipeg: Fernwood Publishing, pp 251–64.

Scott, G. and Wright, S. (2012) 'Devolution, social democratic visions and policy reality in Scotland', *Critical Social Policy*, vol 32, no 3, pp 440–54.

Scottish Government (2011) *Child poverty strategy for Scotland*, Edinburgh: Scottish Government.

Secretary of State for Health and the Secretary of State for the Home Department (2003) *The Victoria Climbié inquiry – report of an inquiry by Lord Laming*, Cm 5730, London: HMSO.

Shannon, G. and Gibbons, N. (2012) 'Report of the Independent Child Death Review Group'. Available at: http://www.dcya.gov. ie/documents/publications/Report_ICDRG.pdf

Silburn, R. (1991) 'Beveridge and the war-time consensus', *Social Policy and Administration*, vol 25, no 1, pp 80–6.

Skehill, C. (2004) *History of the present of child protection and welfare social work in Ireland*, Lewiston: Edwin Mellon.

Smith, K. (2007) 'Social work, restructuring and resistance: "best practices" gone underground' in D. Baines (ed), *Doing anti-oppressive practice: building transformative, politicized social work*, Halifax/ Winnipeg: Fernwood Publishing.

Social Justice Ireland (2012) 'Policy briefing: poverty and income distribution', July. Available at: http://www.socialjustice.ie/content/ income-distribution-and-poverty-ireland.

Stead, P. (2008) 'Progressivism and consensus', in J. Osmond (ed) *Unpacking the progressive consensus*, Cardiff: Cardiff University and The Institute of Welsh Affairs.

Streeck, W. (2011) 'The crises of democratic capitalism', *New Left Review*, vol 71, pp 5–30.

Sullivan, M. (2007) 'Post-devolution health policy', in C. Williams (ed) *Social policy for social welfare practice in a devolved Wales*, Birmingham: Venture Press.

Task Force on the Child and Family Support Agency (2012) 'Report of the Task Force on the Child and Family Support Agency'. Available at: http://www.dcya.gov.ie/documents/ChidFamilySupportAgency/TaskForceReport.pdf

Teater, B. and Baldwin, M. (2012) *Social work in the community: making a difference*, Bristol: The Policy Press.

Theodoropoulou, S. and Watt, A. (2011) *Withdrawal symptoms: an assessment of the austerity packages in Europe*, Brussels: European Trade Union Institute.

Toibin, C. (2005) 'At St Peter's', *London Review of Books*, 1 December, pp 3–7.

Tomlinson, M. and Walker, R. (2009) *Coping with complexity: child and adult poverty*, London: Child Poverty Action Group.

Toynbee, P. (2008) 'This frenzy of hatred is a disaster for children at risk', *The Guardian*, 18 November, p 35.

Toynbee, P. (2010) 'Loyal, public service merits more than this cold trashing', *The Guardian*, 24 August, p 27.

Turnell, A. (1999) *Signs of safety: a solution and safety oriented approach to child protection*, London: W.W. Norton.

Tyrrell, P. (2006) *Founded on fear*, Dublin: Irish Academic Press.

United Nations General Assembly (2011) 'Report on the independent expert on the question of human rights and extreme poverty – mission to Ireland, Magdalena Sepúlveda Carmona', 17 May (A/HRC/17/34/Add.2). Available at: http://daccess-dds-ny.un.org/doc/UNDOC/GEN/G11/132/17/PDF/G1113217.pdf?OpenElement

United Way of Toronto (2007) *One city, one heart, one way: Annual report to the community,* United Way, Toronto. Available at: http://www.unitedwaytoronto.com/downloads/aboutUs/AR2007/2007_UWT-AnnualReport.PDF

Walsh, T., Wilson, G. and O'Connor, E. (2010) 'Local, European and global: an exploration of migration patterns of social workers into Ireland', *British Journal of Social Work*, vol 40, no 6, pp 1978–95.

Weiss-Gal, I., Levin, L. and Krumer-Nevo, M. (2012) 'Applying critical social work in direct practice with families', *Child and Family Social Work*, published online, May. Available at: http://onlinelibrary.wiley.com/doi/10.1111/j.1365-2206.2012.00880.x/pdf

Welsh Assembly Government (2000) *Children and young people: a framework for action*, Cardiff: WAG.

Welsh Assembly Government (2002) *Children and young people: rights to action*, Cardiff: WAG.

Welsh Assembly Government (2007) *Rights in action: implementing children and young people's rights in Wales*, Cardiff: WAG.

White, S., Hall, C. and Peckover, S. (2009) 'The descriptive tyranny of the common assessment framework: technologies of categorization and professional practice in child welfare', *British Journal of Social Work*, vol 39, no 7, pp 1197–217.

Wilkinson, R. and Pickett, K. (2010) *The spirit level: why equality is better for everyone*, London: Penguin.

Williams, C. (2011) 'The jester's joke', in M. Lavalette (ed) *Radical social work today: social work at the crossroads*, Bristol: The Policy Press.

Williams, R. (1983) *Keywords: a vocabulary of culture and society* (2nd edn; 1st edn 1976), New York, NY: Norton.

Woodward, R. and Mackay, K. (2011) 'Mind the gap! Students' understanding and application of social work values', *Social Work Education*, published online, October. Available at: http://www.tandfonline.com/doi/abs/10.1080/02615479.2011.608252